普通高等教育"十一五"规划教材·艺术设计系列

环境|艺术设计 专业英语教程

Environmental Art Design English Textbook

（英汉对照）

◎ 李冬 主 编

◎ 苏波 江慧敏 副主编

化学工业出版社

·北京·

内容提要

本书采用中英文对照的方式，对于室内设计和园林景观设计行业里常用的设计理念、技巧、程序，以及常用的材料、做法和设计、施工中经常涉及的相关方面进行了全面而简要的叙述。其中包括室内家居设计、庭院设计、住宅区景观规划设计、商业区整体规划例讲、展示空间设计、景观小品设计等内容。

本书可作为高等学校环境艺术、景观设计、风景园林等专业学生的教材及相关专业人士参考。

图书在版编目（CIP）数据

环境艺术设计专业英语教程 Environmental Art Design English Textbook（英汉对照）/李冬主编.—北京：化学工业出版社，2009.4（2023.1 重印）

普通高等教育"十一五"规划教材·艺术设计系列
ISBN 978-7-122-04936-0

Ⅰ.环… Ⅱ.李… Ⅲ.环境设计-英语-高等学校-教材 Ⅳ.H31

中国版本图书馆CIP数据核字（2009）第027960号

责任编辑：尤彩霞　　　　　　　　　　装帧设计：史利平
责任校对：洪雅姝

出版发行：化学工业出版社(北京市东城区青年湖南街13号　邮政编码100011)
印　　装：涿州市般润文化传播有限公司
720mm×1000mm　1/16　印张9¼　彩插2　字数182千字　2023年1月北京第1版第9次印刷

购书咨询：010-64518888　　　　　售后服务：010-64518899
网　　址：http://www.cip.com.cn
凡购买本书，如有缺损质量问题，本社销售中心负责调换。

定　　价：38.00元　　　　　　　　　　　　　版权所有　违者必究

Preface　　　　　　前　言

With the development of economy and the extent of opening-up to the outside world, people have more chances to contact and exchange ideas with foreign people and demand for higher environment at quality. There fore the call for special English in environmental art is increasing every year.

Our graduates find it is difficult to catch up with the new trend of environmental art design for 2 reasons: i. their low level of English, ii. their limited vocabulary of technical terms. Therefore, Our book is a material edited to meet this need, based on our experiences of special English education and knowledge of modern indoor and outdoor environmental art design.

In this textbook, we tried to include the main content of indoor and outdoor design, such as home design, which is a typical branch of indoor design with various styles. We set chapters for exhibition design and outdoor environmental design. In addition, garden, residential area, business quarter and landscape elements designs are also included in this book. We tried to cover all the aspects in landscape design.

We tried to arrange the order of the chapters according to the students'

随着经济的发展和对外开放程度的提高，人们对于室内外环境质量的要求越来越高，对外交流和联系的范围也越来越广，人们在生活中对这方面英文知识的需求逐年增加。

在环境艺术专业的应用中，接触外文资料和国外设计的机会越来越多，很多毕业生反映有两个因素限制了个人的发展：其一是英文水平不够高，其二是在学校里面专业外语的学习接触面太窄，专业词汇贫乏，跟不上日益发展的设计市场。在这种情况下，我们根据多年专业英语教学的经验，结合当前室内外环境设计专业发展的新动向，编写了本教材。

本教材囊括了室内外设计的相关内容，室内设计中以最为典型的家居设计为代表，对于各种风格流派均有涉及，并为展示空间设计单列一章，也应时代要求采用更大篇幅讲解室外环境设计。本教材以比较有代表性的庭院设计、居住区景观规划设计和城市商业区环境规划设计作为切入点，并将景观小品设计作为单独的一章，比较全面地覆盖了景观环境设计的各个方面。

本书采取从事设计时最容易入手的思维方式来安排各章节的顺序，

thinking modes, which is easy for them to start and give a simple and comprehensive overview from different levels. Taking the indoor home design for example, we start from explaining design orientation and concept, then make relevant procedures, and complete details at last. We supply many choices to overcome the difficulties in material selection, color usage and lighting design.

We pay great attention to basic knowledge and theories in this book, while we also introduce relevant practical design cases and some recent design pictures. We tried our best to teach English vercabulary in a friendly way with cases and pictures, so that special words can be comprehended and memorized easily. We hope this book will benefit college students, specialists and readers who involve in environmental art, landscape design and landscape gardens.

Landscape design is experiencing rapid development, whose theoretical and practical activities are very active and constantly deepening. During the writing period of this book, inevitable errors and deficiencies may exist because of limited time and author's knowledge level. Corrections and advice are welcom from relevant experts, peers and readers.

Sincerely,

The Authors

January 2009

兼顾各个层面的叙述，力求浅显易懂、全面系统。如室内家居设计中，首先阐述设计定位、设计理念，然后制定相关程序，完善设计细节，在此程序中融入了与设计相关的各种问题，如材料的选择、色彩的应用和照明设计。

本书重视基本知识和基础理论的阐述，并在此基础上联系实际案例以及插图进行配合说明，尽力方便读者阅读和领悟并记忆词汇，力求做到图文并茂、内容新颖。希望能对系统学习环境艺术、景观设计、风景园林等相关专业的院校学生、专业人员和广大读者有所裨益。

景观设计作为一门新兴学科正经历着飞速发展的阶段，学科的理论和实践活动都异常活跃，而且处在不断深化的过程中，本书由于时间和篇幅有限，以及作者的水平所限，疏漏之处在所难免，真诚希望相关专家、同行及广大读者给予指正。

编者　谨识
2009年1月

CONTENTS

目　录

Chapter 1
Indoor Design

第1章
室内家居设计

1.1 Design Orientation

The designer can only decide his design orientation after he collects enough information, such as the host's age, family members, interests and fondness, work nature, living habits etc. before carrying out indoor design.

The interior design plan includes decoration of ceiling, floor and walls, selection of doors and windows, and arrangements of furniture and fabric decorations, which have a lot of principles, rules, and knowledge. He also needs to notice that home is a place for living and personal activities, besides environmental hardware. Therefore, indoor design will always focus on the person and family members living in the room. It is far beyond the regular patterns that designers should grasp the temperament transmitted directly or indirectly by the space and environment, and make the owner have the sense of belonging. It is designer's mission to understand and achieve this aim.

1.1.1 Style Orientation

A room can be designed in many styles. It cannot be separated from its general style whether it is gorgeous or elegant, modern or classical, warm or cosy. It shows an appropriate style that people are seeking for their own.

Style orientation should be suited to the dwellers because suitableness makes one feel comfortable. Most people prefer modern style for its concise lines and bright colors. Such style of decoration taking the principle of natural and

1.1 设计定位

在做一个家居设计之前，我们首先应当了解主人的年龄、家庭人员组成、兴趣爱好、工作性质、生活习惯等基本内容。只有了解了这些基本内容，设计师才能有一个明确的定位和设计方向。

室内设计不仅仅是对天花、地面、墙壁的装饰，门窗的设计选择，以及家具、布艺和装饰品的布置，这些工作有着许多需要遵守的法规、规范，或可以遵循的知识及规律。除了作为环境硬件外，家，更是一个用来居住、充满了个人行为的场所。因此，设计的基本着眼点永远是：生活其间的人，生活其间的家庭。如何通过一个空间环境向参观者直接或间接地传递某种气质，令使用者对环境产生归属感，则是远远超出规范之外的东西。理解并实现这个目标，便是专业设计师的使命。

1.1.1 风格定位

室内设计风格很多，在一个设计中各部分设计不能脱离总体风格，无论是华丽优雅、现代经典、亲切温馨、或是别致个性，都说明人们在寻找着属于自己适合的设计。

风格的定位要适合居住者，合适才舒服，多数人喜爱的是线条简洁、色彩明快的现代风格。现代风格的装饰装修设计以自然

fluent spatial sense conciseness and practicality, and advo cating human-orientation, tries to makes human in harmony with space. Therefore, style orientation should take such factors as the owner's personality, cultural background etc. into consideration.

1.1.2 Function Zoning

The living room is an essential part of all function zones. The first impression of living room is so important that visitors may learn of the owner's taste and self-restraint. As a result, the general style of living room should be unified and integrated with personality, making individuality in accordance with the unity. The living room, as the center to meet guests, receive audio-visual enjoyment, and talk, is the most highly utilized and biggest living space in daily life at home. It is essential to separate living room from meal area nearly by floor, ceiling, partition wall, and color. In a living room, sofa is a material subject for friends and family to talk and get together. Whether it is comfortable or not will impact on the guests' spirits and the atmosphere greatly. Therefore, furniture arrangement in the living room should be carefully considered.

Living room has multi-function usage, which is a big space to hold activities and guide crowds. Therefore, we should first take route guidance and function zones into consideration and arrange furniture reasonably, and then collocation of lights and colors as well as some other auxiliary functions, that is, function before form.

1.1.3 Color Selection

Color tone of a house should be decided according to different styles as well as lighting and reflection of colors. In a house, it is better to have no more than three colors. Color here refers to the color system in which red, yellow, and

流畅的空间感为主体，倡导以人为本，以简洁、实用为原则，努力使人与空间完美和谐。风格的定位要参考主人的性格、文化等因素。

1.1.2 功能分区

客厅作为功能分区中的主要部分，它给人的第一印象很重要。客人可以通过客厅的风格，了解主人的品位及涵养，所以，要使其与整体风格统一，并融入个人的性格，使个性寓于共性之中。客厅是居家生活中使用率最高，也是最大的生活空间，是会客、视听、聚谈等活动的中心。如果客厅与餐区距离很近，可以通过地面、顶面、隔断以及颜色等做好分区，保证客厅使用功能不受影响。沙发是朋友和家人交流、聚谈的物质主体，因此，沙发舒适与否，对客人的情绪和气氛都有重要的影响，因此，要仔细考虑客厅家具摆设的位置。

由于客厅具有多功能的使用性、面积大、活动多、人流导向、相互交替等众多特点；因此，在家具配置设计时，应当合理安排，充分考虑人的导向线路以及各功能区域的划分。然后再考虑灯光色彩的搭配以及其它各项客厅的辅助功能设计，先功能后形式。

1.1.3 颜色的选择

房间的色调要根据风格特点而定，还要考虑采光以及颜色的反射程度。一个空间的颜色最好不要超过三种。这里指的是色系，比如，红、黄、蓝和黑、白、灰

blue, or black, white, grey are not included. If you think three kinds of colors are not enough, you can make improvement by modifying gray scale and saturation. Color tone is mainly reflected through colors of floor, walls and large pieces of furniture with decorations. Different colors bring different effects depending on how they are used and collocated.

Different colors give people different feelings. For example, blue, green and gray make people feel "calm and cool", while red, pink and brown make people feel "warm and excited". Bright colors seem to make the room larger, so they are often used to decorate smaller and dimmer rooms, while dark colors to decorate bigger rooms. Two or three colors of the same kind used harmoniously can achieve a certain effect. For example, the colors of blue, green or gray used together can produce an exquisite and quiet effect. A proper collocation of colors makes room or house as a unified whole and seem spacious. After the choice of a basic tone, a much brighter or dimmer color can be applied to smaller areas, which will make a small room or apartment with decoration lines form delightful contrast. Surely, you can also choose colors with sharp contrast, such as bright against dark, warm against cold, which will make the room vibrant with life.

1.2 Design Procedures

Indoor design is a relatively complex design system with pluralistic factors such as science, art, function, and aesthetics, which concerns varieties of technologies and arts in design theory and practice. Therefore, in the process of designing, it must obey rigid scientific procedures, which in a broad sense refer to all the arrangements from design conception to execution of the design project, while in a narrow sense only refer to the arrangement of the designer putting the ideas in his mind into blueprint for a project.

不算色。如果觉得三个颜色太少，可以调节颜色的灰度和饱和度。色调主要是通过地面、墙面以及大件家具来体现，装饰品只起调剂、点缀的作用。不同的颜色有不一样的效果，主要看怎么利用和搭配。

不同的色彩给人的心理感受是不一样的，比如，蓝、绿、灰色让人感到"安静、凉爽"；红、粉红、棕色使人感到"温暖兴奋"；明亮的色调使房间显得较大，常用来装饰较小、较暗的房间；暗淡的色调使空间显得收敛，常用来装饰较大的房间。二到三种相近色调的颜色搭配，如蓝、绿或灰色，可产生精巧安静的效果。色彩搭配得当，可使房间或房屋浑然一体，显得宽敞。对大面积地方选定颜色后，可用一种比其更亮或更暗的颜色来渲染较小的面积。此方法也可用于有装饰线的小房间或公寓，更能相映成趣。当然，设计时也可以选用具有强烈对比效果的色彩，如亮对暗、暖色对冷色，可以达到生机盎然的效果。

1.2 设计程序

室内设计是一个相对复杂的设计系统，本身具有科学、艺术、功能、审美等多元化要素，在理论体系与设计实践中涉及相当多的技术与艺术门类，因此在具体的设计运作过程中必须遵循严格的科学程序。这种设计上的科学程序，在广义上是指从设计概念构思到工程实施完成全过程中接触到的所有内容安排；在狭义上仅限于设计师将头脑中的想法落实为工程图纸过程的内容安排。

1.2.1 The Drawing Procedures

In this process, the major forms of expression include freehand drawing, plane figure, elevation drawing, sectional drawing, joint detail drawing, perspective drawing and axonometric drawing. Freehand drawing is mainly used for drafting plane function layout and spatial image idea. The perspective drawing is the best expression of indoor special visual image design project. Nowadays people often adopt freehand and computer drawing, which are carriers of space and expressing design purpose. The drawing procedures of indoor design are basically set according to the process of design thinking. Generally, it consists of three periods—conception design, project design and operation design.

1.2.2 The Operation Procedures of the Indoor Design

It is composed of the following procedures: making of the design plan, social investigation and study of project contents, project conception design and specialized coordination, setting of the plan and working drawing design, choice of materials and construction supervision. Among these procedures the project conception design, the setting of the plan and the working drawing design are closely related to our current design education.

(1) Design Plan

The foundation of a design is the data possession rate. Whether you have done an all-round investigation and made a transverse comparison, whether you have searched for large quantities of materials and sorted them out, whether you have found the former inadequacies and problems and made an analysis and supplement, this help the designer who has a vague idea and doesn't know what to start with has a clear ider make it clear. For example, if you

1.2.1 图面作业阶段

在这个阶段采用的表现方式主要包括：徒手画、平面图、立面图、剖面图、细部节点详图、透视图、轴侧图。徒手画主要用于平面功能布局和空间形象构思的草图作业；透视图则是室内空间视觉形象设计方案的最佳表现形式。对表现图的表现方式现在多采用徒手绘制和计算机制作两种方式，两者都是说明空间和表达设计意图的载体。室内设计的图面作业程序基本上是按照设计思维的过程来设置的。它一般要经过概念设计、方案设计和施工设计三个阶段。

1.2.2 室内设计的项目实施程序

这一程序由以下几个步骤组成：设计任务书的制定、项目设计内容的社会调研、项目概念设计与专业协调、确定方案与施工图设计、材料选择与施工监理。其中项目概念设计、确定方案与施工图设计与我们现行的设计教育结合紧密。

（1）设计规划阶段

设计的根本首先是资料的占有率，是否有完善的调查，充分的比较，大量的搜索资料，归纳整理，寻找欠缺，发现问题，进而加以分析和补充，这样的反复过程会让设计师从模糊和无从下手状态当中渐渐清晰起来。举例：电脑专营店的设计，首先应了解其经营的层次，属于哪一级别的经销商而确定设计规模，确定设

环境艺术设计专业英语教程

make an indoor design for an exclusive agency for the sale of computers, first you should make your content of design according to distributor level. After having acquainted yourself with the proportion of its staff distribution, managing pattern, managing ideal and brand advantages, you can decide the design scope even vaguely. The data collection and analysis period should include the following actions: a transverse Then compare and investigate of other design modes of a similar space, acquiring the existing problems and some experiences, such as the shop's location and its traffic transportation, then decide how to use public facilities and how to solve the problems decide the software facilities according to the general customer's range. Investigate the employee turnover and work distribution and a reasonable plan of the route. In this period, a reasonable elementary design concept, that is, the artistic expression orientation, should be put forward.

(2) Brief Analysis

A perfect and ideal spatial function analysis graphics should be put forward in design planning stage. This is an absolutely reasonable function plan free from the confinement of the practical plane. It is for the sake of avoiding the designer's first impressions in perceptual thinking. Sometimes it is a confinement that you do not think so. The existing plane does contain a certain design thoughts, which will inevitably absorb you in it. Once the foundation is well-prepared, then comes the design period in a real sense. It is vital to do some field work and make some detailed measurements, for the spatial imagination of the drawing greatly differs from practical spatial feelings. Knowledge of pipeline and light will help you to narrow the gap between the design and its practical effects. In this period you should

计范围。了解公司的人员分配比例，管理模式，经营理念，品牌优势，来确定设计的模糊方向。比较和调查其他相似空间的设计方式，取得已知的存在问题和经验，例如其位置的优劣状况，交通情况，决定如何利用公共设施和如何解决不利矛盾。参考顾客的大致范围而确定设计的软件设施。考察人员的流动和内部工作，合理地规划路线。这些在资料收集与分析阶段都应详细地分析与解决。这一阶段还要提出一个合理的初步设计概念，也就是艺术的表现方向。

（2）概要分析阶段

设计规划结束后应提出一个完善的理想化的空间机能分析图，也就是抛弃实际平面而完全绝对合理的功能规划。不参考实际平面是避免因先入为主的观念束缚了设计师的感性思维。虽然有时你感觉不到限制的存在，但原有的平面必然渗透着某种程度的设计思想，在无形中会让你旋入。当基础完善时，便进入了实质的设计阶段，实地的考察和详细测量是极其必要的，图纸的空间想象和实际的空间感受差别很悬殊，对实际管线和光线的了解有助于你缩小设计与实际效果的差距。这时如何将你的理想设计结合入实际的空间当中是这个阶段所要

combine your ideal design with the actual space. An important characteristic of the indoor design is that there is no perfect but the most appropriate design. Every design is imperfect because it is confined. The aim of a design is to reduce the influences of the unfavorable conditions on the user under the limited circumstances. The process of transforming the ideal plan into practical paper will unavoidably sacrifice secondary space because of confrontation. However, the principle of plane design is focusing on the reasonableness of the whole and the human. The space plan completed next is to perfect the layout of the furniture equipment. A good start contributes to a rapid and natural development of the plan.

1.3 Design Concept Expression

There is no identical view on the decisive factors of a good design. Designers should pay attention to the following two aspects:

First, balance. Designers must follow this principle all the time, because balance is a natural expression of human activities. People try to pursue balance from a toddler learning to walk to boat-driving at adult. It is equally important for the family space that the space layout and the combination of decoration factors are in balance.

Second, imagination. Imagination of design is the same artistic expression with that of poetry without distortion of reality. Imagination, which comes from the combination of time and space, is the reception of message and personal knowledge and cultivation, so it should reflect a person's cognition, viewpoints and degree of command.

The external expression of indoor design concept mainly reflects on the indoor decoration style, which can be generally summarized as follows:

做的。室内设计的一个重要特征便是只有最合适的设计而没有最完美的设计，一切设计都存在着缺憾，因为任何设计都是有限制的，设计的目的就是在限制的条件下通过设计缩小不利条件对使用者的影响。将理想设计规划从大到小地逐步落实到实际图纸当中，并且不可避免地要牺牲一些因冲突而产生的次要空间，全部以整体的合理和以人为主，是平面规划的原则。空间的规划完成后，向下便是完善家具设备布局。有了一个良好的开端的话，向下便可以迅速而自然地进行了。

1.3 设计理念表达

评价设计优劣的决定性因素，至今都没有一个统一的结论。设计师注意以下两个方面的问题：

第一，平衡原则。在着手进行一个空间规划时，必须时刻把握这个原则。因为平衡是人类活动的自然表现，从孩童学步到驾舟乘风破浪，人类的一切自身活动都在努力追求一种平衡。对于一个家庭空间来说，平衡原则也同样重要。空间的布局，装饰元素的组合都需要讲究平衡的原则。

第二，想象力。想象力是如同诗歌一样的艺术表达方式，但决不是对现实的扭曲。想象力应该能够体现出个人对于现实世界的认知、看法以及掌控的程度。想象力来源于时间与空间的组合，来源于信息的接收，来源于个人的知识与修养。

设计理念的外在体现主要是家居装饰风格的表现，根据风格的大致类型，我们可以简单概括为以下风格类别。

1.3.1 Traditional Chinese style

Chinese tradition upholds solemnity and elegance. Traditional Chinese wooden frame is used to construct indoor decorations such as caisson ceiling, folding screen, partition board etc. The Chinese traditional style always adopts symmetrical spatial drawing manner to achieve a serene, elegant and simple atmosphere.

1.3.2 Local Style

Local style consciously uses local materials and takes a local legend or story as the decorative theme in order to show respect to local traditions and customs and preserve local chara cteristics. It tries to express a leisurely and pleasant rural life in a natural, simple and elegant spatial environment.

1.3.3 Natural Style

Natural style advocates going back to nature and discards artificial materials. It brings wood, bricks and stones, grasses, vines and cloth into indoor design, which is proper and popular in a villa construction.

1.3.4 Archaic Style

With the requirements of modern life having been continuously neeted, people germinate an orientation for traditional, ancient decorations and conventional furniture with artistic value. Therefore, Baroque and Rococo style furniture with beautiful curves and flowing lines is often used as indoor furnishings, accompanied with wallpaper, curtains, carpets, and other housing decorative fabric of the same style, which adds a dignified, elegant and aristocratic atmosphere to the house.

1.3.5 Western Classical Style

This is a pursuit for a gorgeous, elegant classical style. White color tone is set for the room, furniture, doors, and windows. The furniture has classical-style bending legs. A fixed pattern of the traditional western interior decoration is to use all

1.3.1 中国传统风格

中国传统崇尚庄重和优雅，吸取中国传统木架结构来形成室内藻井天棚、屏风、隔扇等装饰，多采用对称的空间构图方式，笔法庄重而简练，气氛宁静雅致而简朴。

1.3.2 乡土风格

主要表现为尊重民间的传统习惯、风土人情，保持民间特色，注意运用地方建筑材料或利用当地的传说故事等作为装饰的主题。在室内环境中力求表现悠闲、舒畅的田园生活情趣，创造自然、质朴、高雅的空间气氛。

1.3.3 自然风格

崇尚返璞归真、回归自然，摒弃人造材料的制品，把木材、砖石、草藤、棉布等天然材料运用于室内设计中。这些做法，在别墅建筑中特别适宜。

1.3.4 复古风格

人们对现代生活要求不断得到满足时，又萌发出一种向往传统、怀念古老饰品、珍爱有艺术价值的传统家具陈设的情绪。于是，欧洲历史上典型的曲线优美、线条流动的巴洛克和洛可可风格的家具常用来作为此类居室的陈设，再配以相同格调的壁纸、帘幔、地毯、家具外罩等装饰织物，给室内增添了端庄、典雅的贵族气氛。

1.3.5 西洋古典风格

这是一种追求华丽、高雅的古典风格。居室色彩主调为白色。家具为古典弯腿式，家具、门、窗漆成白色。擅用各种花饰、丰富的木线变化、富丽的窗帘帷幄

kinds of curlicue, rich changes of wood line, and gorgeous curtains to create a luxury, magnificent and romantic ambience.

1.3.6 Western Modern Style

This style is simple and clear, paying attention to effective use of interior space. It stresses the principle of interior layout based on functional area division making furniture in harmony with the space. It abandons redundant and tedious decorations to emphasize nature and spirit with fashional color and shape.

1.3.7 Japanese Style

This style has an extremely concise space modeling. With a tea table as the center of furniture arrangement, components of grid geometry to echo are used for wooden walls, sliding doors and windows. All these things make the spatial ambience simple, elegant and tender.

1.3.8 Mixed Style (Integration of Western and Chinese Styles)

It pursues modern practical use of spatial structure, while it absorbs traditional characteristics by integrating Chinese and Western styles into one in decorations and furnishings. It will make people feel free and relax with traditional folding screen and tea table, modern-style wall paintings and decorations of doors and windows, new-style sofas together.

Before carrying out detailed design, designers should understand that people of different personalities, cultures, ages and jobs require different styles and characteristics of living environment. The style of the indoor environment must be oriented and created according to the owner's personalities.

1.4 Design Outline and Details

1.4.1 Application of Shapes

A body is made up of surfaces and a surface

是西式传统室内装饰的固定模式，空间环境多表现出华美、富丽、浪漫的气氛。

1.3.6 西洋现代风格

以简洁明快为主要特点，重视室内空间的使用效能，强调室内布置按功能区分的原则进行，家具布置与空间密切配合，主张废弃多余的、繁琐的附加装饰，突出本质和神韵。另外，装饰色彩和造型追随流行时尚。

1.3.7 日式风格

空间造型极为简洁，家具陈设以茶几为中心，墙面上使用木质构件作方格几何形状与细方格木推拉门、窗相呼应，空间气氛朴素、文雅柔和。

1.3.8 混合型风格（中西结合式风格）

在空间结构上既现代实用，又吸取传统的特征，在装饰与陈设中融中西为一体。如传统的屏风、茶几，现代风格的墙画及门窗装修，新型的沙发，使人感受到不拘一格。

在涉及具体案例时，作为设计师应该明白：不同性格、不同文化修养、不同年龄和职业的人其居住空间环境的风格及个性要求是不同的，居家环境风格的营造须结合业主的个性要求进行选择、定位。

1.4 设计要点与细节

1.4.1 形状的运用

形体是由面构成，面是由线

is made up of lines. The lines of the indoor spatial interface and its auxiliary facilities mainly refer to grid lines and lines caused by uneven changes of the surface. These lines can reflect the static or dynamic state of the decorations, the exquisiteness adjust spatial senses and manifest degree of the decorations. For example, dense lines make people get strong sense of direction; groove lines of a pillar can direct people looking up and make them feel as if the pillar is taller and straighter. Straight lines along corridor can make it appear more far-off; the arc grid lines of a theater towards the stage contribute to people's attention towards the stage as arc lines have centripetal or centrifugal force.

The surface of the indoor spatial interface and its auxiliary facilities consists of their respective contour lines and grid lines. Different shapes of surface give people different imagirations and feelings. For instance, a surface with sharp edges and corners gives people a strong and exiting feeling, while a round and smooth surface makes people feel soft and lively; a trapezoidal surface gives people a solid and simple sense, while an orbicular surface with centripetal and centrifugal forces provides a clear focus. As circular and square shapes are neutral, designers often use non-neutral free shapes to create spatial environment of individual character isties.

1.4.2 Application of Patterns in Indoor Design
(1) Function of Patterns

A.Patterns can improve proportion of interfaces or auxiliary facilities through people's visions. A square wall, decorated by a pair of parallels, looks like a rectangle. If its opposite wall is decorated in the same way, the room seems to be profounder.

B.Patterns can provide space with a static or dynamic sense. Grid patterns composed of interlaced lines will fill the space with a stable

构成。室内空间界面和配套设施中的线，主要是指分格线和由于表面凹凸变化而产生的线。这些线可以体现装饰的静态或动态，可以调整空间感，也可以反映装饰的精美程度。例如，密集的线有极强的方向性；柱身的槽线可以把人们的视线引向上方，增加柱子的挺拔感；沿走廊方向表现出来的直线，可以使走廊显得更深远；弧线有向心力或离心力，剧场顶棚弯向舞台的弧形分格线，有助于把人的视线引向舞台。

室内空间界面和配套设施的面是由各界面和配套设施造型的轮廓线和分格线构成的，不同形状的面会给人以不同的联想和感受。例如，棱角尖锐形的面，给人以强烈、刺激的感觉；圆滑形的面，给人以柔和活泼的感觉；梯形的面给人以坚固和质朴的感觉；正圆形的面中心明确，具有向心力和离心力等。正圆形和正方形属于中性形状，因此，设计者在创造具有个性的空间环境时，常常采用非中性的自由形状。

1.4.2 室内设计中图案的运用
（1）图案的作用

A.图案可以利用人们的视觉来改善界面或配套设施的比例。一个正方形的墙面，用一组平行线装饰后，看起来可以像矩形；把相对的两个墙面全部这样处理后，平面为正方形的房间，看上去就会显得更深远。

B.图案可以赋予空间静感或动感。纵横交错的直线组成的网格图案，会使空间具有稳定感；

sense, while oblique lines, broken lines, wavy lines and other strong-directional lines will fill the space with a dynamic sense.

C.Patterns can fill the space with a certain ambience and temperament. For instance, it will make people feel all the components as a whole by wall patterns joining ceiling with floor.

(2) Pattern Selection

A.When selecting a pattern, the designer should adequately consider size, form, function and temperament of the space. Dynamic patterns are better to be applied to entrances, corridors, stairs and other relaxing public places and not be used in bedrooms, living-rooms or other rooms for relaxation. Abstract and exaggerated animal and plant patterns can only be used to decorate adults' rooms, but not children's. Patterns decorated in children's rooms should be more interesting and colorful, while in adults' rooms pure colors should be carefully used so as to provide a stable and unified environment.

B.It is better to apply no more than two patterns in one space. If you select three or more patterns, one of them should be conspicuous than the other two, otherwise it will lead to a visual confusion.

1.5 Material Selection

With increasing environmental pollution, environmental protection has aroused the consumers' attention, who actively use some innoxious decoration stuff and green electrical appliances. In addition, designers can also advise consumers to choose some furniture that can be recycled so as to reduce the use of wood, which will protect the environment and improve the sense of environment protection of the next generation.

斜线、折线、波浪线和其他方向性较强的图案，则会使空间富有运动感。

C.图案还能使空间环境具有某种气氛和情趣。例如，装饰墙采用带有透视性线条的图案，与顶棚和地面连接，给人以浑然一体的感觉。

（2）图案的选择

A.在选择图案时，应充分考虑空间的大小、形状、用途和性格。动感强的图案，最好用在入口、走道、楼梯和其他气氛紧凑的公共空间，而不宜用于卧室、客厅或者其他气氛闲适的房间；过分抽象和变形较大的动植物图案，只能用于成人使用的空间，不宜用于儿童房间；儿童用房的图案，应该富有更多的趣味性，色彩可鲜艳明快些；成人用房的图案，则应慎用纯度过高的色彩，以使空间环境更加稳定而统一。

B.同一空间在选择图案时，宜少不宜多，通常不超过两个图案。如果选用三个或三个以上的图案，则应强调突出其中一个主要图案，减弱其余图案，否则，会造成视觉上的混乱。

1.5 材料选择

随着环境污染的日益严重，环保问题正引起消费者的高度重视，主要表现在消费者积极主动地使用一些无毒、无污染的装修材料，更换绿色电器等方面。另外，设计师也可倡议消费者选购一些可循环利用的材料制成的家具，减少木材的使用，保护环境，对提高下一代环保意识培养起到实际的促进作用。

With development of housing construction and the improvement living conditions, people's requirements for indoor environment is far beyond basic living needs, so the study of ecological design is attracting much more attention. It is an urgent need of many families to introduce ecology to indoor design. Modern living environment requires indoor design to accord with ecological principles and use some natural stuff to create a natural, environment-friendly and energy-saving interior environment.

The development of new stuff has provided indoor design with a plentiful material basis. Designers can take full advantage of different textures of various materials, and make an adequate design to achieve different effects. People have broken the original confinement and are brave in selecting new materials. Considering the demands for materials of indoor design, designers should select materials of good quality and at the same time in harmony with the environment, that is, green materials or materials harmonious with environment.

In the choice of material texture, designers should pay attention to the following points:

1.5.1 Conformity between Matericals and Space in Characteristics

Indoor space determines the space atmosphere, the composition of which is closely related to the personality of materials. Therefore, when people choose materials, they need to choose materials whose personality fit with the atmosphere of space. For example, it is better to use some bright, gorgeous and smooth glass and metal materials in an entertainment and leisure space, giving people a luxury, elegant and exciting feeling.

1.5.2 Full Display of the Inner Beauty of Materials

As natural materials contain so many

住宅建设的发展和居住条件的改善，使人们对室内环境的要求已超越了基本生活需求的层面，生态设计的研究备受重视。把生态引入室内设计，是千家万户的切身需要。现代生活的居住环境要求室内设计符合生态学的观点，运用基本无毒无害的纯天然材料和绿色建材，创造出回归自然、环保节能的室内环境。

新材料的拓展赋予室内装饰丰富的物质基础，可以充分利用不同材料的质地特征进行合理搭配，从而可以获得千变万化、不同风格的艺术效果。人们在材料选择上已不拘一格，打破了原有的固定模式去尝试运用新材料。基于室内设计对材料的要求，对"绿色家具"设计的材料而言，则要求选择既有良好使用性能又能与环境相协调的材料，即绿色材料或环境协调材料。

在选择材料的质感时，应把握好以下几点：

1.5.1 材料与空间在性格上相吻合

室内空间的性格决定了空间气氛，空间气氛的构成则与材料性格紧密相关。因此，在材料选用时，应注意使其性格与空间气氛相配合。例如，娱乐休闲空间宜采用明亮、华丽、光滑的玻璃和金属等材料，会给人以豪华、优雅、兴奋的感觉。

1.5.2 充分展示材料自身的内在美

天然材料巧夺天工，自身具备

beautiful elements as pattern, color, texture etc. that cannot be imitated by humans, designers should identify and apply such elements when selecting materials so as to fully reflect their beauty. For instance, the stone of granite and marble, and the wood of Manchurian ash, teak, mahogany, and so on, have a natural texture and color. However, it does not mean that high-grade and expensive materials can achieve good results. On the contrary, the choice of low-prices materials can also get good results, as long as they are made the best use.

1.5.3 Relationship between Material Texture and distance/Space

The same material, when applied to places of different distances or spaces, often gives people different impressions. The material of high smooth gives people stronger feelings, when they are closer. For example, a light metal material, when used in small places, especially as a rim, is dazzling, but when it is applied to a larger area, people often feel rugged. Here is another example: A rubble wall may look rough in a near distance, however, it appears smoother from far away. Therefore, designers should grasp these characteristics and cleverly apply them to different space areas.

1.5.4 Conformity to the Usage Requirements

Spaces of different usage must use suitable materials. For instance, a sound-recording studio or a computer room has the needs of sound insulation and absorption, moisture-proof, fire-proof, dust-proof, light etc., so materials of different textures and properties should be used. Similarly, walls, floors and ceilings in one space should select suitable materials to meet the different requirements for wear-resistance, tolerance, soft illumination level and anti-static etc.

1.5.5 Cost Effectiveness

Designers should consider cost of materials

许多人无法模仿的美的要素，如图案、色彩、纹理等，因而在选用这些材料时，应注意识别和运用，应充分体现其个性美，如石材中的花岗岩、大理石；木材中的水曲柳、柚木、红木等，都具有天然的纹理和色彩。在材料的选用上，并不意味着高档、高价便能出现好的效果；相反，只要能使材料各尽其用，即使花较少的费用，也可以获得较好的效果。

1.5.3 材料质感与距离、面积的关系

同种材料，当距离远近或面积大小不同时，它给人们的感觉往往是不同的。表面光洁度好的材质越近感受越强，越远感受越弱。例如，光亮的金属材料，用于面积较小的地方，尤其在作为镶边材料时，显得光彩夺目，但当大面积应用时，就容易给人以凹凸不平的感觉；毛石墙面近观很粗糙，远看则显得较平滑。因此，在设计中，应充分把握这些特点，并在大小尺度不同的空间中巧妙地运用。

1.5.4 与使用要求相统一

对不同要求的使用空间，必须采用与之相适应的材料。例如，录音棚或微机房需有隔声、吸声、防潮、防火、防尘、光照等不同要求，应选用不同材质、不同性能的材料；对同一空间的墙面、地面和顶棚，也应根据耐磨性、耐污性、光照柔和程度以及防静电等方面的不同要求而选用合适的材料。

1.5.5 注意材料的经济性

选用材料必须考虑其经济

环境艺术设计专业英语教程

and aim at low prices with high efficiency. Even though it is better to decorate a high-end space with materials of high price and grade, it is not proper to use high-grade materials everywhere , otherwise it will give people a vanity and vulgar sense.

1.6 Indoor Color Design

Indoor colors directly influence people's emotions. Scientific application of indoor colors contributes to people's work and health, meet functional requirements and achieve asthetic objective. Rational use of contrast and match can enhance the visual sense of space in indoor environment, and expand or shrink vision. In an interior design, low-intensive colors should be used in main space, while high intensive colors in parts for decoration, which can achieve an elegant visual effect. The combination of cold and warm colors affect indoor arrangement significanthy. A pleasing color helps to reduce people's fatigue. Proper choice and combination of colors can achieve double effects of health and decoration.

1.6.1 Color Harmony

Matching colors is the fundamental issue of indoor design, which is essential for indoor color effect success. One color can not form aesthetic, if it is isolated. You cannot tell good colors from bad ones, but you can easily notice improper color matching. The color effect depends on the interrelationship of different colors. The same color in different backgrounds can achieve different effects, which is due to its unique sensitivity and relevance. As a matter of fact, coordination of colors becomes the key of color matching.

As mentioned above, colors are closely related to psychology and physiology. When

1.6 室内色彩设计

室内色彩直接影响到人的情绪。科学地用色，处理得当才能符合功能要求，有利于工作，有助于健康，获得美的效果。合理运用对比色或调和色的搭配，能在室内环境中加强视觉的空间感，从而达到使视野扩大或缩小的作用。在室内设计中，主体空间应以低纯度的色调为主，然后再以高纯度色彩在局部和重点进行点缀，这样便可以起到典雅丰富的视觉效果。冷暖色调的搭配可以有效影响室内效果的主要因素。赏心悦目的色彩有益于人体疲劳的缓解，恰当的颜色选用和搭配可以起到健康和装饰的双重功效。

1.6.1 色彩的协调问题

室内色彩设计的根本问题是配色问题，这是室内色彩效果优劣的关键，孤立的颜色无所谓美或不美。就这个意义上说，任何颜色都没有高低贵贱之分，只有不恰当的配色，而没有不可用的颜色。色彩效果取决于不同颜色之间的相互关系，同一颜色在不同的背景条件下，其色彩效果可以迥然不同，这是色彩所特有的敏感性和相关性，因此如何处理好色彩之间的协调关系，就成为配色的关键问题。

如前所述，色彩与人的心理、生理有密切的关系。当我们注视

we focus on red for a certain period of time, then turn to looking at a white wall or close our eyes, we will see green. If we take the same bright pure color as the background with a grey area on it, and imagine the background is green, the grey part will look red. The former phenomenon is known as "successive contrast (continuous comparison)" and the latter is "simultaneous contrast". Visual organs, in accordance with the natural physiological conditions, instinctively regulate its stimulation to keep the visual balance. Only when complimentary relationship of colors established, can the visual organs achieve balance. If we observe a mid grey area in the a mid-grey background, there won't appear a visual different phenomenon from the mid grey color. As a result, mid grey is suitable for the balance required by people's visual organs and this is the objective standard of color balance and coordination.

The basic concept of color coordination is formed by white color spectrum, whose wave lengths range from red to purple. These pure colors coordinate with each other. When an equivalent amount of black or white is added to pure colors, they are still coordinated, but uncoordinated with imbalaced amount. For example, beige and green, red and brown are uncoordinated, while sea green and yellow, which are close to pure color, are coordinated. A pair of complimentary colors in the color ring are coordinated. Trisect of the color ring results in a particularly harmonious coordination. It is necessary to use approximate and contrast coordination of colors in the indoor design. The former can give a calm feeling of harmony and unity, while the latter can strike people's heart for it comes from conflict and confrontation of contrast colors. The key lies in the correct control

红色一定时间后，再转视白墙或闭上眼睛，就彷佛会看到绿色。此外，在以同样明亮的纯色作为底色，色域内嵌入一块灰色，如果纯色为绿色，则灰色色块看起来带有红味，反之亦然。这种现象，前者称为"连续对比"，后者称为"同时对比"。而视觉器官按照自然的生理条件，对色彩的刺激本能地进行调剂，以保持视觉上的生理平衡，并且只有在色彩的互补关系建立时，视觉才得到满足而趋于平衡。如果我们在中间灰色背景上去观察一个中灰色的色块，那么就不会出现和中灰色不同的视觉现象。因此，中间灰色就同人们视觉所要求的平衡状况相适应，这就是考虑色彩平衡与协调时的客观依据。

色彩协调的基本概念是由白光光谱的颜色，按其波长从紫到红排列的，这些纯色彼此协调，在纯色中加进等量的黑或白所区分出的颜色也是协调的，但不等量时就不协调。例如米色和绿色、红色与棕色不协调，海绿和黄接近纯色是协调的。在色环上处于相对地位并形成一对补色的那些色相是协调的，将色环三等分，造成一种特别和谐的组合。色彩的近似协调和对比协调在室内色彩设计中都是需要的，近似协调固然能给人以统一和谐的平静感觉，但对比协调在色彩之间的对立、冲突所构成的和谐和关系却更能动人心魄，关键在于正确处理和运用色彩的统一与变化规律。和谐就是秩序，一切理想的配色方

and use of color unity and changes. Harmony is order, so that all the ideal color schemes, adjacent light and color layouts are the same. Seven harmonious permutations can be found on the color solid.

1.6.2 Indoor Color Composition

Color often plays a special role in indoor composition.

(1) Color can attract or distract people's attention to an object.

(2) Color can make an object appear larger or smaller.

(3) Color can strengthen or destroy the form of indoor space. For example, in order to break the monotonous hexahedral space, designers can use super planar art methods, which are independent with the division and confinement of the ceiling, walls and floor. The composition of space becomes blury and broken by freely and randomly color composition.

(4) Color can decorate through reflection. Because of various materials, texture, and form of indoor objects, and their levels of diversity and complexity in space, indoor color uniformity apparently lies in the first place. Generally varieties of colors can be summed up as follows:

Walls, floor and ceiling occupy a large area and play the roles of setting up all the objects in the room. Background color takes priority over the other issues and selections in indoor color design.

Different colors in different background have different influences on the nature of the room, people's psychological perception and emotional reactions. Although a special color may be fully applicable to the ground, but the result is different if it is used on the ceiling. Here is a brief analysis of different colors used on the ceiling, walls and floor:

案，所有相邻光色的间隔是一致的，在色立体上可以找出7种协调的排列规律。

1.6.2 室内色彩构图

色彩在室内构图中常可以发挥特别的作用。

（1）可以使人对某物引起注意，或使其重要性降低。

（2）色彩可以使目的物变大或变小。

（3）色彩可以强化室内空间形式，也可破坏其形式。例如：为了打破单调的六面体空间，采用超级平面美术方法，它可以不依天花、墙面、地面的界面区分和限定，自由地、任意地突出其抽象的彩色构图，模糊或破坏了空间原有的构图形式。

（4）色彩可以通过反射来修饰。由于室内对象的品种、材料、质地、形式和彼此在空间内层次的多样性和复杂性，更重要的是兼顾室内色彩的统一性。一般可归纳为下列各类色彩部分：

如墙面、地面、天棚，它占有极大面积并起到衬托室内一切对象的作用。因此，背景色是室内色彩设计中首要考虑和选择的问题。

不同色彩在不同的空间背景上所处的位置，对房间的性质、对心理知觉和感情反应可以造成很大的不同，一种特殊的色相虽然完全适用于地面，但当它用于天棚上时，则可能产生完全不同的效果。现将不同色相用于天棚、墙面、地面时，作粗浅分析：

Red Ceiling: Disturbing and heavy.

Wall: Invasive and forward.

Ground: Attractive and alert.

Pure red is always used as emphasis color, which is very rare and should be limited, otherwise it will make the space complicated.

Pink Ceiling: It depends on personal taste whether this color will be elegant, pleasing and comfortable or too sweet.

Pink Wall: Weak, too sweet if it is not belong to gray tone.

Pink Ground: Too delicate (very rare).

Brown ceiling: Boring.

1.7 Illumination Design

It is said that "Only after going through light exposure that buildings can come to alive." It is obvious that light plays an integrated role in physical, physiological, psychological and aesthetic aspect, as main media between people and space. Lighting is not only a necessary condition for life, but also constitutes basic elements of visual aesthetics. Different forms of lighting will influence objects' or space image, color tone and people's impression. Lighting can create or damage the atmosphere of an indoor environment.

To create a comfortable lighting environment, first of all, it is needed that reasonable distribution of illumination, appropriate indoor surface reflectivity, soft lighting and no dazzling glare. Secondly, the lighting specifications, such as size, power, shape, quality, structure, color and materials, should be fit perfectly for the decoration style. In addition, we should also attach importance to "security, applicability, cost-effectiveness and handsomeness." In short, the art of indoor lighting not only has a direct impact on the indoor atmosphere, but also influence people's physiology

红色，天棚：干扰，重；墙面：进犯，向前；地面：引人注意、警觉。

纯红除了当作强调色外，实际上是很少用的，用得过分会增加空间复杂性，应对其限制更为适合。

粉红色，天棚：精致，愉悦舒适，或过分甜蜜，决定于个人爱好；墙面：软弱，如不是灰调则太甜；地面：或许过于精致，较少采用。

褐色，天棚：沉闷。

1.7 照明设计

有人曾说："建筑物必须经过光线的照射，才能产生生命"，光线作为人与空间之间的主要媒介，具有物理、生理、心理和美学等综合作用。照明不但是进行生活的必要条件，同时亦是构成视觉美学的基本要素。不同形式的照明会左右物体或空间的形象、色调以及它们给人留下的印象。照明既能营造也能破坏室内环境的气氛。

创造一个良好的使人感到舒适的照明环境，首先，需要照度分布合理，室内各个面的反射率适当，光线柔和且无刺眼的眩光。其次是灯饰的规格、尺寸、功率、造型、质量和结构、颜色、材质要与装修风格完美地吻合。另外，还要注重"安全、适用、经济、美观"。总之，室内照明艺术不仅直接影响到室内环境气氛，而且对人们的生理和心理产生影响。在进行室内照明设计时，应根据

and psychology. Designers should determine the lighting layout, source type, shape and matching methods based on the applicable features of indoor space environment. Efficient combination of visual effects and artistic ideas, and proper use can create a harmonious ambience and mood, fully reflect the style of the space and enhance the art of architecture. In this way, it meets people's aesthetic demands and exerts their mental and visual functions to improve the indoor lighting art and people's life quality.

1.7.1 Lighting Function

The designer should use different types of lighting systems to meet requirements of three main objects: people, architecture and important items(such as works of art and collections). How to provide light for people should be set in the first place in these three main objects.

1.7.2 Background Lighting

Background lighting can fill room with soft and lively light to make space more humane. In order to obtain ideal background lighting, modern lighting design employs satisfactory reflection of light by walls and ceilings, and avoids producing a bright spot or shadows on a person's face. Background light can come from wall lamps, pendant lamps or some other high light sources of a cupboard or pillars etc.

1.7.3 Decorative Lighting

The role of luxuriant pendant lamps and candlestick-shaped wall lamps is to show false impression, that light is providing from background, by flashes of light. Such lighting systems must be accompanied with auxiliary lighting, other wise the entire space only with decorative lighting sytems will be too dazzling.

1.7.4 Accent Lighting

Accent lighting is a delicate light beam on a

室内空间环境的使用功能、视觉效果及艺术构思来确定照明的布置方式、光源类型、灯具造型及配光方式。这三者的有机结合和正确使用，才能创造出室内空间环境彼此协调一致的气氛和意境，充分体现建筑空间的风格，增强建筑艺术的美感，从而满足人们的审美要求和视觉心理机能，达到提高室内照明艺术和生活质量的目的。

1.7.1 照明的功能

策划住宅照明的时候应注重运用不同类型的照明装置，从而满足以下三要素对光线的需求：人、建筑和重点物品（如艺术品、收藏品等）。这三个要素都很重要，但重中之重是考虑如何为使用空间的人提供照明。

1.7.2 背景照明

背景照明的光线使房间充盈着柔和、迷人的气氛，令空间人性化。为获得理想的背景光线，现代的照明设计采用反射自墙面和天花板的光线，这样就可以避免产生亮点，光线也不会在人的脸上产生阴影，从而达到令人满意的光线效果。背景照明的光线可以来自壁灯、吊灯或在橱柜、梁柱等高处光源。

1.7.3 装饰照明

华丽的吊灯、形似烛台的壁灯的任务是使其照射的表面闪烁炫耀，造成给房间提供背景光线的错觉。这种照明须有层次分明的辅助照明作为陪衬，因为如果将装饰照明装置作为房间的全部光源，会使整个空间显得过于耀眼。

1.7.4 重点照明

重点照明采用精心布置的较

particular object, such as works of art, bonsai or some details of constructions to achieve artistic effects. Accent lighting are not designed from a bright light source like a candle or a wall pendant lamp. It always adopts embedded, track or movable lighting.

1.7.5 Working Lighting

Working lighting is a high-intensity lighting system for people, who have to focus their eyes in working or some other activities, such as lights and table lamps in pharmacies, long strip lights below cabinets or on sides of the mirror in the bathroom.

为集中的光束照射某件物体、艺术品、盆景或某些建筑细部结构，主要目的是取得艺术效果。重点照明的设计常常使观赏者觉得光线是不太明亮的光源提供的，比如蜡烛或墙上的吊灯。嵌入式可调节照明装置、跟踪照明设备或可移动照明装置都可以提供重点照明的光线。

1.7.5 工作照明

工作照明是人们做用眼较多的工作或活动时需要的非常集中的高亮度光线照明。像药房中常用的灯、台灯、安装于橱柜下面的长条状照明灯、或者浴室中镜子两侧竖直安置的长条状灯具都可提供工作照明。

Chapter 2
Courtyard Design

2.1 Layout of Courtyard Design

The creation of courtyard atmosphere is up to the layout plan of courtyard design. A reasonable layout can make a small graden rich and full of fun, while a big garden filled with a good gratation. When designing a courtyard, we should obey the following principles.

2.1.1 Unified Diversity

Many aespects in courtyard design should follow the principle of unity, such as form and style, gardening materials, color and lines etc. We preferred the garden to be regarded as a whole from main theme to details, but we do not like rigid atmosphere because of over unification. That is why we often describe it as unified diversity, which means to seek unity in changes.

Nowadays, there are three popular courtyard styles in the world:

(1) Natural–style

Garden designs were influenced by the pursuit of natural basic daily necessities after the 20th century with the slogan of "back to nature". Chinese-style garden should be regarded as the originator of natural-style garden, for it pursues elegant and secluded nature with vibrant and vigorous plants.

(2) Western–style

Known as regular courtyard, western-style garden is a symmetrical and graceful landscape layout with an axis and grand scale,

2.1 庭院设计平面布局

庭院的平面布局设计关系着整个庭院氛围的营造，合理的布局可以使小面积的庭院变得丰富而有趣味，使大面积的庭院层次丰富不空洞。在做庭院平面设计时，我们应当遵循以下原则：

2.1.1 多样统一原则

"统一"的原则，用在庭院设计中所指的方面很多，例如形式与风格、造园材料、色彩、线条等，从整体到局部都要讲求统一，但过分统一则显呆板，疏于统一则显杂乱。所以常在统一之上加一个多样，意思是需要在变化之中寻求统一，免于成为不伦不类的风格。

目前世界上主要流行以下三类风格庭院：

（1）自然式庭院

20世纪人们提出了"回归自然"的口号，衣食住行都狂热地追求自然，这股风潮自然传播到了庭院设计中来。其实中国式园林自古以来就以幽雅自然、僻静清幽为胜，植物多为自然生长形态，一石一木都追求其自然风貌，可称之为自然式庭院的鼻祖。

（2）西式庭院

又称规整式庭院，多为对称式景观布局，有中轴线，植物多被人工修葺成几何形，容易形成

whose plants are pruned to be geometric-shaped. It is more and more popular at current times with significant development, resulting in a large area of unnatural man-made artificial landscapes.

(3) Mixed Style

Originally, natural and regular styles are mutually contradictory, but it has been very common to see both these styles in one garden, as the improved lady Cheongsam in the fashion industry. It is a new trend to combine Chinese and western style in one design, so we still need a long time to prove its advantages and disadvantages, similar to the other styles.

2.1.2 Balance

The sense of balance is an overall sense of objects' weight on both sides from a person's visual center. If there are a couple of objects of the same weight and size in the front—let's imagine they're a couple of stone lions, people will have a sense of balance. However, the lack of any one would cause visual imbalance. The designer should pay attention to this principle in the courtyard design.

2.1.3 Proportion

It is necessary to consider the proportion of every part in the courtyard, such as the proportion between a part and the whole courtyard, or even proportion between a small piece of wood or stone and the environment. As people's facial or body features, it is easy to be noticed, if non-conforming proportion appears in courtyards, which won't be treated as "beauty".

2.1.4 Rhythm

Rhythm refers to the repetition of similar rhymes in accordance with a certain rule in music or poetry. Courtyard design should also take this into consideration, for visitors can get a sense of rhythm only after a clever use of a variety of synchronized rhythm.

规模庞大、宏伟雍容的风貌。在现行经济发达的社会中，这种庭院设计风格逐渐兴盛起来，而且愈演愈烈，以致形成大面积人为造作的非自然景观。

（3）混合式庭院

本来自然式与规整式是相互矛盾的，但目前自然式与规整式在同一庭院内混合应用已经相当流行，就像时装界的改良旗袍，中西结合的设计正在蔓延。一种设计风格的形成需要很长时间，同样，我们仍需要很长时间来辩证这种风格的优缺点。

2.1.2 均衡原则

均衡感是人对其视觉中心两侧景物的整体分量感。如果前方是一对体量与质量相同的景物，假设是一对石狮，即会产生均衡感，缺失一个便是视觉失衡。庭院设计中也要注意这一原则。

2.1.3 比例原则

庭院中到处需要考虑比例的关系，大到局部与全局的比例，小到一木一石与环境的小局部。一旦失去比例，观赏者很容易发觉。正如人面部的五官或躯体，比例适当就可尊称为"美人"，反之类推。

2.1.4 韵律的原则

在音乐或诗词中按一定的规律重复出现相近似的音韵即称为韵律。设计庭院也是如此，只有巧妙地运用多种韵律的同步，才能使游人获得韵律感。

2.1.5 Contrast

In courtyard design, one local landscape desplayed together with another one whose shape, color, texture etc. are in controst with those of the former one will creat a sharp visual contrast and at the same time give tourists a clear aesthetic taste.

2.1.6 Harmony

Harmony refers to a sense of dynamic unity with the color, shape, line of a scene in time and space. Winter scene should be paid more attention to avoid visual emptiness, because most ornamental plants are withered in winter. As a result, evergreen plants will be a better choice in winter.

2.1.7 Texture

Texture refers to thickness and sense of biological and non-biological organisms in the courtyard. For example, soft lawn, and deep green moss can make people feel reluctant to step on or even to touch them. If we put a smooth rock in the river sand, a harmony scene will be generated by these landscape elements of the same texture and features.

2.1.8 Simplicity

Simplicity used in courtyard design means a simple elegant arrangement of scenery. Courtyard design pursues and imitates natural beauty, which needs to be refined to artistic beauty. Just as what western gardeners said "Simplicity is beauty", choices should be made under the simple and elegant principle.

2.1.9 "Human Viewing Human"

"Human viewing human" is a new topic developed with ethological theory in recent 20 years, which is directly applied to courtyard design. That is to say, the most eye-catching design principle in courtyard design should consider the "human" behavior first. A good design should be

2.1.5 对比原则

在庭院设计中，为了突出园内的某局部景观，利用体形、色彩、质地等与之相对立的景物与其放在一起表现，以造成一种强烈的视觉对比效果，同时也给游人一种鲜明的审美情趣。

2.1.6 和谐原则

和谐是指庭院内的景物在变化统一的原则下，色彩、体形、线条等在时间和空间上都给人一种和谐感。尤其值得注意的是冬季景色的布置，因为多数观赏性植物都在冬季凋零，造成视觉空洞，因此，庭院植物在种植时应种些常青植物。

2.1.7 质地原则

质地是指庭院中生物与非生物体表面结构的粗细程度，以及由此引起的感觉。如细软的草坪、深绿色的青苔均匀而细腻，让人舍不得去踩碰，如果在旁边一片河沙中放一块光润的顽石，这一组质地相近的景物显然会呈现协调之美。

2.1.8 简单原则

"简单"一词用在庭院设计中是指景物的安排以朴素淡雅为主。自然美是庭院设计中刻意追求和模仿的要点，自然美被升华为艺术美要经过一番提炼。正如西方造园家提出"简单也是美"的道理一样，应当在朴素淡雅的原则之下取舍。

2.1.9 满足"人看人"原则

"人看人"成为行为学的理论是近20年来才提出的新课题，而且直截了当地引申到庭院设计中来。也就是说，庭院设计中最引人注目的设计原则应当首先考虑"人"的行为问题。一个好的设计

able to sensitively respond to the needs of people, amuse them as much as possible, raise their spirits, and keep interest in other people's activities in or near the courtyard meeting their behavioural needs.

2.1.10 Pursuit of Artistic Conception

Such works of art as courtyard will be a recreation place for visitors, once it becomes a habitat. A charming courtyard can attract visitors to come for several hundreds of years. This shows that the image of creativity and fun has triggered the visitors' thinking and imagination, in other words, They have sensed an "artistic mode", which is mainly reflected as follows:

(1) Poetic charm——People often say "One's emotion is roused by the scene." It means people's emotion are roused by, also including imagination and fantasy what they see.

(2) Picturesque scene——Courtyard is the body of the picture, which should be pleasant enough to satisfy visitors strolling in it.

2.2 Courtyard Style Design and Orientation

2.2.1 The Needs of Family Members

The first step to create a beautiful courtyard is to make a good plan. First of all, the designer should set the courtyard style according to environmental conditions, family composition and maintenance ability. The garden style can reflect the way of life of a family. If the family consists of a couple of office workers, it is better to plant some flower trees or perennial flowers in the courtyard, because they are too busy to take care of them. For the family with children, it is better to lay a lawn to place toys and plant some colorful annual or biennial herbaceous flowers and flower bulbs; if someone in the family is interested in plant maintenance and management, they can plant some seasonal herbaceous flowers,

应当能对人的需要最敏感地做出反应，使人尽情地游玩，使他们精神焕发，并对庭园内部或周边的其他人的活动保持兴趣盎然，满足他们行为的需要。

2.1.10 寻求意境原则

庭院这类艺术品在成"境"之后就成为欣赏者游乐之所。一座耐人寻味的庭院可连续几百年成为游人的乐往之地，可见创作的形象和情趣已经触发游人的联想和幻想，即体会到了"意境"，突出表现为：

（1）诗情——常说"见景生情"，意思是有了实景才触发情感，也包括联想和幻想而来的情感。

（2）画意——庭院是主体的画卷，对于庭院中自由漫步的游人来讲，只有"八面玲珑"才能使人满意。

2.2 风格的选择与定位

2.2.1 家庭成员的需要

营造一个美丽庭院的第一步就是要做好规划设计。首先应决定庭院的风格，要根据环境条件、家庭人员组成及养护能力等情况制定计划。庭园样式也可反映出居住在这里的家庭的生活方式。如果是上班族夫妇的两口之家由于无暇养护花草，庭院中常常只种些花木或宿根花卉；有幼儿家庭的庭院则应铺设可放玩具的草坪，并种植一些色彩艳丽的一、二年生草花和球根花卉；如果家中有人对植物养护管理感兴趣，就可种些四季时令草花，营

thus build a perfect ornamental garden. In short, courtyard style and cultivation of plant species should be based on composition and age structure of the family.

There are various garden styles, whose basic forms are generally based on the owners' preferences. As referred before Garden styles can be simply divided into three categories— regular(Western), natural(Chinese) and mixed style. At present, private courtyard styles can be divided into four basic schools: Chinese and Japanese styles in Asia, French and British styles in Europe. Buildings have various styles and types, such as the gap between classical and modern, the contrast between avant-garde and traditional, the differences between Eastern and Western. Choice of garden type is often made according to the building style. In the past, typical Japanese-style courtyards, such as garden-style courtyard and tea courtyard, often integrate natural scenery with the garden, giving people a sense of quietness and elegance. However, Japanese-style courtyard and western-style buildings can not be harmonized, while Japanese-style architecture is also incompatible with the regular courtyard style, therefore designers should take into consideration the harmony between garden style and building. For those who love simplicity, they can plant some grasses and flowers in the yard or make a green plant nursery. If you want to achieve a more desirable landscape effect, you may ask professional designers to design and decorate your courtyard. For example, winding roads with tall trees on both sides will make people feel that "The courtyard is deep." and curve-shaped arches, carved railings, and banister with carefully pruned bushes will be showing a European style.

2.2.2 Courtyard Color

Color is one of the factors influencing the courtyard style. One technique of color design is to decide the main hues of the garden based on

建一个完美的观赏花园。总之，庭院样式及所栽培植物种类应根据家庭人员组成与年龄结构有所选择。

庭院有多种不同的风格，一般是根据业主的喜好确定其基本的样式。前面将庭园的风格样式可简单地分为规则式（西方式）和自然式（中国式）及混合式三大类，目前从风格上私家庭院可分为四大流派：亚洲的中国式、日本式，欧洲的法国式和英国式。而建筑却有多种多样的不同风格与类型，如古典与现代的差距、前卫与传统的对比、东方与西方的差异。常见的做法多是根据建筑物的风格来大致确定庭园的类型。过去具有典型日本庭院风格的杂木园式庭院与茶庭等，往往融自然风景于庭园之中，给人清雅幽静之感。但日式庭院与西式建筑两者难以统一，而且与规则式庭院也有格格不入之感，因此要考虑到庭园风格与建筑物之间的协调性。崇尚简洁的可以在庭院中种些花草，或者是做成一个绿色植物的苗圃。而如果希望取得更加理想的景观效果，许多人会请专业的设计师来设计和制作庭院。如用曲折小道配合高大树木让人产生"庭院深深"的感觉；而用曲形拱门、雕花栏杆、立柱配合精心修剪的矮丛植物，则会呈现出欧陆风情。

2.2.2 庭园色彩

庭园色彩也是影响庭园风格的因素之一，对色彩规划的一个技巧是根据建筑色彩与周围环境

the colors of buildings nearly. Foliage plants are very important in garden design, and it is natural in the United Kingdom and the other European countries to plant some foliage plants in flower beds. Variegated-leaf-plant, such as species with white spots, imbedded in green leaf-plant, are brighter than pure green species, for example senecio cineraria and Asagiri Haocao with silver leaves can set the flower bed even brighter. Other color-leafed plants with orange, red or purple leaves can form a sharp contrast increasing the brightness of the hue. In addition, differences of leaf shapes and texture can also be taken into consideration.

Summer is a season when many varieties of plants are flourishing; therefore, we can apply diverse color combination and use wild perennial flowers to embellish the garden. In summer, it will not give people a sense of clutter, even though we use a combination of several different bright-colored flowers. For example, we can use some bright-colored snapdragons of different color tones to make several lively color blocks, and we can add some silver-leaf plants or white-flower sweet alyssum to neutralize the effect.

2.2.3 Impact of Garden Drainage and Light

Drainage, light, ventilation, soil, and so on will affect plants' growth, especially whether light is sufficient or not is an important condition to determine the choice of flowers. Generally speaking, the ideal place to build a garden is the place heading south with enough sunshine. Therefore, the designer should first make it clear the geographical conditions of the villa garden, for example the sunshine time in one day, the location of sunny and shady sides etc. On this basis, we can choose suitable species in such environment. However, we can also build a garden on shady side.

2.2.4 Courtyard Area

A larger house has more choices of garden

确定庭园的主色调。观叶植物在花园的设计中很重要,在英国等欧洲国家,认为花坛中栽种些观叶植物是很自然的事情。绿色中嵌有白斑的斑叶植物比纯绿色种类明度高,如叶菊、朝雾蒿草等,可将花坛衬托得更明亮,其他另栽具有橙色、红色及紫色叶的彩叶植物,可形成强烈的对比,增加色调的明快感。此外,还可考虑叶形的变化、质感的差异等。

夏季是一个开花植物种类繁多的季节,因此,可以进行多样化的色彩组合,用充满野趣的多年生草花来点缀。在夏季即使用色彩明度高的多种花色组合也不会有杂乱之感。例如可以用艳丽的、不同色系的金鱼草配成多个活泼的色块,这其间可以点缀一些银叶植物或白花香雪球等加以中和。

2.2.3 庭园排水与光照条件的影响

排水、光照、通风、土质等会影响到植物生长发育,特别是光照充足与否是决定可栽培花卉种类的重要条件。一般来说,光照条件好、朝南的地方是花园建造最理想的位置,所以必须首先弄清别墅庭园的地理条件,如一天中的日照时间、阴面与阳面的位置等。在此基础上选择适宜这些环境的植物种类。背阴处也能建设富有特点的庭园,如可建成阴地花园以供观赏。

2.2.4 庭院面积的大小

面积较大的宅院可以选择的

styles, because the larger the area is, the more plant species can be chosen, then the more complex the collocation will be. However, we must consider consistency of the whole when planting trees and flowers and avoid conflict between them. A small house only has limited applicable area, so we should make a careful plan and plant less species.

2.3 Courtyard Plant Design and Classification

2.3.1 Domestic

The overall layout of Chinese gardens requires deepness and adjacent emptiness, stresses "isolated scene" and "hidden scene" in space, and demands circulation and endlessness to create infinite charm in a limited space. In the creation of plant landscape, Chinese gardens strive for personification of plants, trying to integrate poetic and scenic charm. It often uses plant to name buildings and garden scenic spots. Finally, in respect of plant configuration, Chinese gardens need more woody plants and less herbaceous plants to reproduce the state of plant shapes creating landscapes.

2.3.2 Abroad

(1) Japanese-Style Courtyard

The Japanese-style courtyard is composed of the Zen garden, Circuitous tour garden and tea tao garden.

The Zen garden basically uses no flower plants, because it mainly pursues spiritually the extreme state of "cleanness, emptiness and nothingness". Circuitous tour garden is abundant in varieties of plants, for example, small stem maple which grows slowly, five needles pine with good shapes, small arbor of various appearances, shrubs and short plants covering on the rocks as well as podocarpus marcophyllu, Japanese hemlock and evergreen rhododendron. Evergreen

庭园风格也较广泛，因为面积越大可选的植物种类也越多，搭配方式也可复杂一些，但在种植时必须顾及到整体的一致性，避免相互冲突。而狭小的宅院可用面积有限，因此须有周密的配置计划，所栽植的植物种类应少一些。

2.3 庭院植物设计与式样分类

2.3.1 国内

中国园林的总体布局，要求庭院重深，处处邻虚，空间上讲求"隔景"、"藏景"，要求循环往复，无穷无尽，在有限的空间范围内营造出无限的意趣；在植物景观的创造方面讲究植物的拟人化，力求将植物的诗情画意写入园林；并用植物来命名建筑或园林景点；最后在植物配置方面，要求木本植物应用多、草本植物应用少，重现植物形体造景的状态。

2.3.2 国外

（1）日式庭园

日式庭园可分为枯山水庭院、回游式庭园和茶道庭院。

其中枯山水庭院，园内基本上不使用任何开花的植物，它主要是在精神上追求"净、空、无"的终极状态。而茶道庭园中植物种类非常丰富，有株干不大、生长缓慢的槭树；有造型优美的五针松；形态多姿的小乔木；有丛生灌木和覆盖于岩石之上的地被植物以及罗汉松、日本铁杉和常

plants not only can preserve the landscape appearance of the garden, but also can provide a green background for bright-colored flower plants and leaf plants, which makes the garden more colorful. Circuitous tour garden, absorbing the gardening characteristics of the Zen garden and the tea tao garden, combines the garden landscape of four seasons and the quiet and natural scenery of rural atmosphere. It amazes people by the elegance and quietness of plant shapes and the charm and gracefulness of plant colors, reflecting the nature and wildness which Chinese gardens is lack of.

(2) Italian-Style Courtyard

As the Italian peninsula borders on seas from three sides and is abundant in mountains and hills, gardens are often built on slopes. From buildings to the outside, the control of orderly shapes is lessened, which is special for its plants distribution, merging gardens into natural scenery. In early times, there were many plant species in the garden, while later people attach more importance to the beauty of the plant itself. Erect and emerald green podocarpuses are often used as wayside trees or planted in rows; umbrella pines with conical crowns are used as background trees and are the most special plants in the garden. In plain areas, we can use carefully trimmed Chinese boxes to form a geometric pattern as green fences, and form a flower bed dividing flower plants and leaf plants.

(3) French Regular Style

French gardens have terrace garden layout, due to the influence of the Italian regular garden-building arts. However, as the terrain in France is flat, the French garden layout scale appears grander and more magnificent. People trim trees, build flower beds and plant plenty of flowers. On the verge of good-shaped trees, seasonal blooming flowers are planted as a rim, which become an embroidered-style flower bed. On the lawn of a big area, people plant shrub flowers and grasses to form various textures and patterns.

绿杜鹃。常绿植物不仅可以保持园林的景观风貌，也可为色彩明亮的观花或色叶植物提供一道绿色背景，而使园林色彩更为丰富多彩。回游式庭园吸取枯山水和茶道庭园的造园特征，将庭园的四季观赏性景观与静谧自然的乡土气息的风景融为一体，惊诧于其植物形体的高雅、沉静，以及植物色彩的生动多姿，显示出中国园林所缺少的天然和野趣。

（2）意大利式庭园

由于意大利半岛三面濒海，多山地丘陵，因而其园林建造在斜坡上，从建筑物开始，向外逐渐减弱整齐图形的控制，而融于自然环境之中，在园林植物的配置上独具特色。早期的庭园中植物种类繁多，以后注重植物本身的个性美。罗汉松挺拔苍翠，常作为林阴树或列植；伞松具有圆锥形树冠，作背景树，是庭园中最富特色的植物。在平坦地带运用整形的黄杨等作矮绿篱构成几何形图案，将花木分开，形成植坛。

（3）法国规整式

法国园林受到意大利规整台地造园艺术的影响，也出现了台地式园林布局，但法国地势平坦，在园林布局规模上，显得更为宏大而华丽。剪树植坛，大量地运用花卉，在造型树的边缘以时令鲜花镶边，成为绣花式花坛，在大面积草坪上，以栽植树木花草来镶嵌组合成各种纹理图案。

(4) British Natural Style

The Great Britain is a country of hills, whose climate is warm and humid. Natural style is the main style of British garden. Red geranium, blue Chinese lobelia and yellow calceolaria are commonly used in gardens of this style.

2.3.3 Problems in Courtyard Design

(1) No clear main point. Overemphasize pavement on the ground and the pavement is not harmonious with buildings. It appears more disordered when many hard materials are used.

(2) Each corner of the garden has become a center and everywhere is stuffed with top-notch gardening works. This problem is a common fatal habit, because we buy materials on impulse without considering their size and applicability. All these stuffs are placed in the garden, which together with plants will make the garden in disorder and without any characteristic at all.

(3) Most people will buy their favorite plants from the gardening center on impulse or accept the whole potted plant or a cupping given by friends or relatives as a gift. Therefore, people will place them freely without considering their needs and size because of too many plants.

(4) Bad matching. Plants are bad matched, as a result the courtyard appears to be disordered and too similar without individuality or too complex.

(5) People mechanically copy foreign courtyard styles without considering the courtyard's practical scale and shapes as well as the local climate and geographical location.

2.4 Matching of Courtyard Plants

It is called 'plant storage' by landscape experts due to improper match of courtyard and plants, or mess growth of plants. In order to avoid

（4）英国自然式

英国是一个丘陵国家，呈缓坡丘陵。气候温暖多湿，从客观条件上促使其园林形成自然风景式。其庭园花卉主要用红色的天竺葵、蓝色的半边莲、黄色的蒲包花。

2.3.3 庭院植物设计中易出现的问题

（1）没有明确重点。过分注重铺地，并且铺装与建筑不协调。用了许多种硬质材料后，更显得凌乱。

（2）处处都是重点。花园的每一个角落都成了中心，到处都塞满了园艺精品。这个毛病是我们养成的一个致命的习惯，光凭一时冲动就把东西买回来了，全不考虑它的大小和是否适用。充斥在花园里的，除了植物外，还有许多的东西，结果，许多花园变得杂乱无章、毫无特色可言。

（3）随意选择和摆放植物。大多数的人都会凭一时冲动将自己喜欢的植物从园艺中心购买回来，或是接受朋友或亲戚馈赠的整盆植物或插枝。如此来说，植物多了，其结果就常常是植物随意摆放，没有真正地考虑过庭院的需求而影响景观。

（4）搭配不当。植物搭配粗放不精细，庭院显得杂乱无章，形式过于雷同，缺少个性或太过复杂。

（5）照搬照抄其他风格。没有根据庭院的实际规模、形状以及本地的气候和地理位置，就直接照搬照抄国外的庭院风格。

2.4 庭院植物搭配

庭院和植物搭配不当，植物种植混乱，在园林专家的眼里把这看做"花草仓库"。为了避免庭

disorder of plants and forming plants storage, we can arrange plants layout by following methods in details.

A courtyard has various original shapes such as square, rectangular, wide-flat, long or narrow. You'd better make a plan of courtyard usage—having a rest for a while or just walking through. Then you can decide the combination ways of laying bricks and virescence. For virescence, one should pay attention to arrangement of tall and short plants and color match. Besides, a courtyard is an extension of the indoor environment, and both sides should be in harmony with each other in aspects of visual effects and functions.

2.4.1 Gate and Trees

The gate is like a person's face and is significant for courtyard design. Concerning of this, Japan's green garden designers have created a lot of beautiful works: the combination of a certain number of trees to create a certain feature, or planting more trees to make a green fence, and many designs making use of a hidden gateway to give the courtyard gate a sense of depth.

2.4.2 Gate and Moss

Soft moss often reminds us of carpet under our feet. As a result, if the approaches to courtyard are covered with green moss, it will give guests a warm feeling of pleasure. Generally, in addition to the trails, the earth's surface should be covered with moss, and sometimes some high ground is also covered by moss achieving the effect of a small hill. However, it is not appropriate to grow moss in dry areas, so the design is limited to humid environment.

2.4.3 Trails and Trees

As trails in a garden is for walking, the role of trees is to give people a peaceful and cozy feeling. Some trails are designed plain and simple, but the others are designed with careful thoughts: they can be either clustered by roadside

院沦落为花草仓库,我们通过以下的细节处理手法来组织庭院植物布局。

庭院的初始形状有多种,正方形、宽扁或窄长,庭院的主要作用也能用于停留坐卧或是只需穿行往来两种,依此来确定硬地铺装和绿化的结合方式。绿化的部分注重层次,注意高矮搭配和色彩搭配。另外,由于庭院是室内环境向外的延续,在进行植物搭配时应当注重庭院和室内二者从视觉效果和功能上的互相配合。

2.4.1 大门和树木

大门好比人的脸,对庭园设计有着非同寻常的意义。有鉴于此,日本的绿色庭园设计师们创造了很多优美的门廊作品:或利用一定数量的树木组合营造某种主体特征;或种植为数较多的树木做成绿色栅栏,很多设计实例利用隐蔽玄关门廊给予庭园大门一种深邃感。

2.4.2 大门与苔藓

苔藓的柔软常令我们想起地毯,因而如果在庭园道路附近覆盖绿色苔藓,那会给予宾客愉悦温馨的感觉。通常除了行走的小径外,地表都应铺满苔藓;也可覆盖部分高地,产生一种小山坡的效果。但是,苔藓不宜在干燥地区生长,所以设计只局限在湿润的气候环境下。

2.4.3 小径和树木

庭园小径的主要作用是供游人散步,可以利用树木给予散步的人祥和安逸的感觉。小径的设计可以单纯朴素,也可多费些心思,例如路边簇拥灌木丛或伴随

bushes or accompanied by flower beds. Garden path and plants design clearly reflect the owner's unique taste of life.

2.4.4 Main Courtyard and Trees

Most of the trees in a garden are planted with care and good maintenance, whose pretty form is a good reproduction of the Japanese garden model of the old era. In some cases, carefully trimmed bushes play a role of setting off other trees in the garden. In recent years, the use of artificial modification of trees in the garden design particularly the use of ordinary hardwood, such as Zamu, has been common practice, However, Zamu maintenance is not an easy task. When garden is divided into several parts, or have geometric shapes on the ground, tall trees and shrubs will become very important design factors. To some extent, trees are often the main materials to split garden.

2.4.5 Small Courtyard and Trees

Bamboos are more common used in a small garden, because of their beautiful, tall and straight trunks. Landscape of small space is most vividly designed by using vertical lines.

Garden experts say that we can use scientificity, culture, practicability and artistry to evalue the performance of the courtyard design, but this is too professional for the owner of the courtyard. Whether a garden can achieve a good effect depends on the master's interest.

2.4.6 Functions of Courtyard Plants

(1) Security

In personal environment, people need to occupy and control certain space. Psychologists believe that space not only provides a relative sense of security and ease of communication, but also is a symbol of the owner's identity and power. As a result, the sense of space control has already existed from ancient time and is

花坛。庭园小径和树木的设计应能清晰地体现主人独特的人生品味。

2.4.4 主庭和树木

大部分庭园中的树木栽植在护理保养过的园地中，俊逸的造型很好地再现了旧时代日本庭园的模式。在某些实例中，精心修剪的灌木丛起到了为庭园树木作陪衬的作用。近年来，使用经人工修饰的树木在庭园设计中已蔚然成风，尤其使用普通的落叶树，如杂木，然而，杂木的保养实非易事。每当庭园被划分成若干部分，或者在园地上制作几何图形，高大的树木和园地的灌木都会成为非常重要的设计因素。在某种程度上，树木常常是分割庭园的主要材料。

2.4.5 小庭和树木

较小的庭院更多地选用毛竹，自然的落叶类植物因具有俊美挺拔的树干而备受青睐。小空间的景观在垂直的线条中被设计体现得淋漓尽致。

园林专家说，虽然可以用科学性、文化性、实用性和艺术性来衡量庭院设计的好坏，但对于院子的主人来说这未免太专业，庭院能否有个好效果，关键要看主人的兴趣是否在这儿。

2.4.6 庭院植物的作用

（1）安全性

在个人化的空间环境中，人需要能够占有和控制一定的空间领域。心理学家认为，领域不仅提供相对的安全感与便于沟通的信息，还表明了占有者的身份与对所占领域的权力象征。所以领域性作为环境空间的属性之一，古已有之，无

everywhere. Garden plant arrangement design should respect this personal space, so that people can get a sense of stability and security. For example, ancients often planted Basho against the inside of walls, which have no trunk, but stretch softly. It is more difficult for thieves to climb, and it arouse the sense of thicker wall at the same time. Another example, green barriers are very common in the private garden as a division tool in the courtyard and safety suggestion for the family members. The green barriers have achieved the family's respective spatial constraints thus makes people get a sense of area control.

(2) Practicality

Originally, the ancient courtyard was an economical and practical orchard, medicinal herbs garden or vegetable garden. Actually nowadays in many private courtyards or villa gardens, we can still see beautiful scenery of fruit trees or a pastoral vegetable bed. We can even see some people who enjoy a more refined life doing some gardening work themselves, such as planting some fragrant sanitarian grasses, trees or flowers in their courtyard. In fact, whether in a home garden or a green space outside, functions of each green land should be diversified. It should not only have plants for entertainment and sightseeing, but for use, participation and protection of visitors, because participation provides people with a sense of satisfaction and enrichment. Adding stools to the tree shade will provide a rest place for people; opening of the lawn can allow people to enter; building gardens and horticultural facilities can provide visitors the chance of participating in gardening activities. Using shrubs as fences has several functions, which can not only divide the big land into small functional areas, but keep out wind, reduce noise and hide indecent scenery to form a visual control. At the same time for the shrubs are

处不在。园林植物配置设计应该尊重人的这种个人空间欲望，使人获得稳定感和安全感。如古人在家中围墙的内侧常常种植芭蕉，芭蕉无明显主干，树形舒展柔软，人不易攀爬上去，种在围墙边上，既增加了围墙的厚实感，又可防止小偷爬墙而入；又如私人庭院里常见的绿色屏障既起到与其他庭院的分割作用，对于家庭成员来说又起到安全感的暗示作用，通过绿色屏障实现了家庭各自区域的空间限制，从而使人获得了相关的领域性。

（2）实用性

古代的庭院最初就是经济实用的果树园、草药园或菜圃。甚至在现今的许多私人庭园或别墅花园中仍可以看到满园硕果，或者是有着田园气息的菜畦。更有懂得精致生活的人，自己动手进行园艺操作，在家中的小花园里种上芳香保健的草木花卉。其实无论在家中庭园还是外面的绿地，每一块绿地上的植物功能都应该是多样化的，不仅针对游赏、娱乐，而且还应具有供游人使用、参与以及生产防护等功能，使人获得满足感和充实感。在冠荫树下增加座凳给人提供休息场所；草坪开放就可让人进入活动；设计花园和园艺设施，游人就可以亲自动手参与园艺活动；用灌木作为绿篱有多种功能，既可把大场地细分为小功能区和空间，又能挡风、降低噪声，隐藏不雅的景致，形成视觉控制，同时栽培低矮的观赏灌

low plants, people can view their shapes, flowers, leaves and fruits closely.

(3) Agreeableness

In modern society, it is not enough to confine plant landscape to economic utility, which must also be beautiful, attracting and agreeable to satisfy people's aesthetic and psychological needs of love for beautiful things. An individual plant has its own beauty of shape, color, texture, seasonal changes and so on. Through combinations of such elements as shape, line, color, texture as well as a reasonable scale, coupled with background elements of green land (paving, terrain, buildings, urban element etc.), plants growing in clusters or groups can not only beautify the environment and enrich the landscape design, but also can help people regulate emotions and cultivate sentiments unconsciously in their aesthetic enjoyment.

(4) Privacy

Privacy can be understood as the selective control of the approaching degree of personal space. People's choice of private space can be expressed as hope of being alone, having personal space, or free space of a few people from the others' interference, or intention of name concealing from the public. In the highly competitive and rushed social environment, especially in a prosperous city, people have a great desire to own a quiet place far from clamor of the city. Such requirements can easily be met in family yards and gardens, or natural green space decorated with designed plants. Plant design is the best natural element to create a private space. Designers consider people's needs of privacy, which does not mean they will design a completely closed space, but make a complete and clear limit on space based on the attributes of

木，人们可以接近欣赏它们的形态、花、叶、果。

（3）宜人性

在现代社会里，植物景观仅仅只局限于经济实用功能是不够的，它还必须是具有美感的，动人的，令人愉悦的，必须同时满足人的审美需求和人们追求美好事物的心理需求。单株植物有它的形体美、色彩美、质地美、季相变化美等；丛植、群植的植物通过形状、线条、色彩、质地等要素的组合以及合理的尺度，搭配不同绿地的背景元素（铺地、地形、建筑物、小品等），既可美化环境，为景观设计增色，又能让人在潜意识的审美感觉中调节情绪，陶冶情操。抓住人微妙的心理审美过程，对于创造一个符合人内在需求的环境起到十分重要的作用。

（4）私密性

私密性可以理解为个人对空间可以接近程度的选择性控制。人对私密空间的选择可以表现为一个人独处，希望有适合自己个性的环境，或几个人亲密相处不愿受他人干扰，或者反映个人在人群中不求闻达、隐姓埋名的倾向。在竞争激烈、匆匆忙忙的社会环境中，特别是在繁华的城市中，人类极其向往拥有一块远离喧嚣的清静之地。这种要求在家庭的庭院、花园里容易得到满足，而在大自然的绿地中也可以通过植物设计来达到的要求。植物设计是创造私密性空间的最好的自然要素，设计师考虑人对私密性的需要，并不一定就是设计一个完全闭合的空间，但在空间属性上要对空间有较为完整和明确的限

space. Some green fences with a rational lay-out or some scattered trees can provide privacy and people can read, sit quietly, chat and talk privately in the quiet environment created by plants.

(5) Publicity

As human need private space, sometimes they also need public open space. Environmental psychologists once put forward the social centripetal and centrifugal space concepts, so in the same way green land of a garden can also be divided into centripetal and centrifugal green space. The former includes the city square, park, green space in the center of a residential area etc. Square trees of large crowns should be planted to provide shade for people, lawns should not be as open as possible and shelters should also be set. Plant varieties in residential areas should be of high ornamental values such as foliage plants, flower plants, fruit plants, and so on. These design ideas are inclined to help people get together to promote their interaction and to seek more information.

2.4.7 Garden Plant Design Trends

An American designer said: "The garden design is a plant material design in the final analysis, whose purpose is to improve human's living environment, and other contents can only function in an environment with plants." Plants are the only element of vitality in the garden and are closely related to people. A few years ago, "turf hot" and "color plant cover" was very popular. Because they have such defects as low ecological benefits, landscape patterning and higher maintenance costs, they are limited to be used in local areas now. The trend of modern garden plant design will be more particular about eco-efficiency. The design will focus on the diversity of plant species, for each plant has its specific biological features, ecological habits

定。一些布局合理的绿色屏障或是分散排列的树就可以提供私密性，在植物营造的静谧空间中，可以供人们读书、静坐、交谈和私语。

（5）公共性

正如人类需要私密空间一样，有时人类也需要自由开阔的公共空间。环境心理学家曾提出社会向心与社会离心的空间概念，园林绿地也可分绿地向心空间和绿地离心空间。前者如城市广场、公园、居住区中心绿地等，广场上要设置冠荫树，公园草坪要尽量开放，草坪不能一览无余，要有遮阳避雨的地方，居住区绿地中的植物品种要尽量选择观赏价值较高的观叶、观花、观果植物等。这些设计思路都是倾向于使人相对聚集，促进人与人相互交往，并进而去寻求更丰富的信息。

2.4.7 庭院植物设计发展趋势

一位美国设计师说过："园林设计归根到底是植物材料的设计，其目的是改善人类的生活环境，其它的内容只是在一个有植物的环境下才能发挥出来。"植物是园林要素中唯一具有生命力的物质，与人息息相关，前些年曾流行一时的"草坪热"、"彩色地被"终因其生态效益低、景观模式化、维护费用高等缺陷而限制在局部区域使用。而现今的庭园植物景观设计发展趋势将更讲究生态效益。在进行设计中将做到植物种类的多样化，每种又都有其特定的生物学特征、生态习性及观赏

and ornamental characteristics. We can create a comfortable and beautiful living environment full of vigor by making use of seasonal aspects, physical changes, color changes regional characteristics, and humanization, variability of combinations, and diversity of the landscape. Secondly, we can create unexpected results with the combination of Chinese plant culture, modern aesthetic point of view and high-technology.

2.5 Main Points of Small Courtyard Design

①A theme is necessary, which should be fully expressed. (Such as walls, pavement, plants etc.)

②Pavement style can neither be single nor be too many. Generally, it is better to have two or three types in a private courtyard,

③There should be a clear space division and make full use of the Chinese garden artistic conception.

④Plant cultivation should be natural which is better to be exquisite instead of being greater in quantity with density and a reasonable combination.

⑤Common landscape elements such as water, pavilion, wooden platforms, flower racks, open space and haugh, etc.

⑥The park road should be smooth with adequate twists and turns, and terrain changes can be properly used to divide space.

⑦The landscape structure should be focused on: shape of walls and application of materials, landscape walls, and decoration.

特性，利用植物季相、形体变化、色彩变化等方面的特性及植物的地域性、亲人性、组合的多变性、景观的多样性等特点，创造各种富有生机、舒适而美观的人居环境。其次，结合中国植物文化以及现代人的审美观点和高科技条件，创造出人意料的效果。

2.5 小庭院设计要点

① 要有主题，充分表现主题。（如围墙、铺装、植物等表现）

② 铺装样式不能单一，但样式也不能太多，一般私家庭院2～3种为佳；

③ 空间划分清晰，充分运用中国园林意境思想；

④ 植物种植形式以自然为主，宜精不宜多，疏密结合，合理搭配；

⑤ 常见的造景元素：水、亭、木平台、花架、休憩空间、汀步等；

⑥ 园路流畅，曲折有度，可适当利用地势变化来划分空间；

⑦ 应注重立面景观构造：围墙的造型和材料运用、景墙、装饰等。

Chapter 3
Planning and Design of Residential Area

第3章
住宅区景观规划设计

3.1 Concept

Residential area is a region with high housing concentration, and a certain number of public services and utilities. It is a community to supply residents with housing, open space and services in daily life, consisting of a number of residential quarters or several living groups.

3.1.1 Location

The so-called "Spirit of Place" is a feature of social activities conducted in space. From the perspective of social development, the objective of residential area planning (including urban planning) is to form a good community by providing some places in terms of constructions of material morphology and a good interpersonal relationships on the level of broad exchanges.

3.1.2 Concept and Purpose

Design of residential areas should fully take such requirements into account as people's needs, its role and impact on the environment, construction and operation cost, and requirements of landscape image,etc. It should take the strategy of sustainable development as the guidance and follow the general principles of community development, ecological improvement and sharing community. It also need to follow the corresponding planning and design principles of residential areas to construct a civilized living community suitable to live in. Starting from meeting the needs of people, residential planning should take full account of the habitability of living environment, identification and ownership, and foster a human environment with culture and vitality.

3.1 概念

住宅区是一个城市中住房集中、并设有一定数量及相应规模的公共服务设施和公用设施的区域，是一个在一定地域范围内为居民提供居住、游憩和日常生活服务的社区。它由若干个居住小区或若干个居住组团组成。

3.1.1 定位

所谓"场所精神"便是一种在空间中进行的社会活动的特征。住宅区规划（包括城市规划）从社会发展的角度来看其目标是通过物质形态构筑为人们提供一些场所，建构一种广义交流层次上的良好的人际关系，期望形成一个良好的社区。

3.1.2 设计理念及目的

住宅区规划设计应该全面考虑满足人的需求、对环境的作用与影响、建设与运营的经济性以及景观形象的塑造等要求，以可持续发展战略为指导，遵循"社区发展、生态优化和共享社区"的总体原则以及相应的设计原则，建设文明、适居的居住社区。从满足人的需求出发，住宅区规划应该充分考虑居住环境的适居性、识别性与归属性以及营造具有文化与活力的人文环境。

3.2 Main Points of Space Design

3.2.1 Space Constitution

Buildings and urban spaces are limited by three-dimensional material elements. The space issue considered by residential planning mainly focuses on external space research, and on how to create a suitable living environment through external space construction.

The constitution elements of external space can be divided into basic elements and auxiliary elements. The basic elements refer to buildings, tall trees and other large-scale structures(such as walls, columns, large and tall natural terrain, etc.), that limit main space. The auxiliary elements are usually refer red to the three-dimensional entities of smaller-scale to form a subsidiary space or to enrich the basic space scales and levels, such as low walls, the courtyard gates, steps, shrubs and undulating terrain, and so on.

3.2.2 Traffic Analysis

Traffic function is the basic function of various accesses of residential areas. Choices of resident trip mode and transportation mode directly influence all the types of layout and connection forms of accesses at all levels in the residential areas. Although with the influence of economic development, living habits, natural conditions, ages, income and other factors, the choices of transportation modes have various characteristics due to residents of different regions, ages and levels, but they still have general laws.

According to the means of transport, traffic modes can be divided into three kinds, motorized traffic, non-motorized traffic and pedestrian traffic. The basic factor considered by residents is traffic distance when selecting traffic modes. There are three factors that influence the correlativity between traffic distance and traffic modes, physical ability, traffic time and transportation costs. Different people lay special

3.2 空间设计要点

3.2.1 空间构成

建筑与城市空间由三维的物质要素限定而成。住宅区规划设计所考虑的空间问题，主要侧重于研究外部空间，并研究如何通过外部空间的构筑营造一个适居的居住环境。

外部空间的构成要素可分为基本构成要素和辅助构成要素。基本构成要素是指限定基本空间的建筑物、高大乔木和其他较大尺度的构筑物（如墙体、柱或柱廊、高大的自然地形等）。辅助构成要素是指用来形成附属空间以丰富基本空间的尺度和层次的较小尺度的三维实体，如矮墙、院门、台阶、灌木和起伏的地形等。

3.2.2 交通分析

通行功能是住宅区各类通路的基本功能。居民出行与区内交通方式的选择直接影响着住宅区各类各级通路的布局与连接形式，虽然受经济发展水平、生活习惯、自然条件、年龄和收入等因素的影响，不同地区、不同年龄和不同阶层的居民所选择的交通方式有不同的特征，但仍然有其一般的规律。

交通方式按采用的交通工具分为机动车交通、非机动车交通和步行交通三种。居民在考虑选择交通方式时的基本要素是交通距离。影响交通距离与交通方式的相关关系的因素有体能、交通时间和交通费用三项。不同的人在其选择时对三类因素考虑的侧重点是不同的。对老年人、儿童

emphasis on the three factors, when making their choices of transportation. To the elderly, children and adolescents, physical ability is the most important consideration. To the low-income people, the cost of their chosen mode of transportation is the main aspect, while for the high-income earners, maybe time is of the highest value. However, in most cases, in a comparatively short distance (usually 500 to 1000 m), most residents will choose walking as their preferred mode of transportation, because it's convenient, within the bearing capacity of physical strength, and needs no costs at all. For a longer travel distance (usually over seven km), it is better to use motor vechles as means of transportation. Within the range of 1-7 km, bicycles will be the main mode of transportation for most of the residents who have a bike, but also because it's convenient, within the bearing capacity of physical strength, and needs a small amount of fixed and immediate cost. For those who do not have a bike yet, and the residents of the elderly and children, they still will use motor vechles as the means of transportation.

3.2.3 Public Facilities

The municipal facilities of residential areas include various types of water, electricity, gas, heating system, communication and sanitation engineering facilities on and under the ground, serving for the residential area only. The planning of such facilities should follow the principles of the overall coordination, management and maintenance, and the principle of sustainable development to save land, energy and water, reduce pollution, improve the ecological environment of the living area and meet the needs of modern life.

The planning of municipal facilities in residential areas should mainly consider their configuration, layouts, land-use arrangements, and the integrated planning of all types of municipal pipelines.

(1) Water–Supply System

Water supplies of residential areas include residents' living water supply, and some other water

和青少年来说，选择交通方式时体能是最主要的考虑因素；对低收入者来说，费用是其选择交通方式的主要方面；对高收入者来说，可能时间对他来说价值最高。但是，在绝大部分情况下，在比较短的距离内（一般为500～1000m），步行是大部分居民首选的交通方式，因为其方便、体力能够承受，而且不产生任何费用。对距离较长的出行（一般在7km以上），应该采用机动车作为交通工具。在1～7km的范围内，自行车交通将会是大部分拥有自行车的居民的主要交通方式，也因为其方便、体力能够承受，而且仅发生极小的、固定的非即时性费用。对那些尚未拥有自行车的居民以及老年人、儿童，他们的出行仍然将采用机动车作为交通工具。

3.2.3 公用设施

住宅区的市政设施包括为住宅区自身供应服务的各类水、电、气、供暖、通信以及环卫的地面、地下工程设施。住宅区市政公用设施的规划应该遵循有利于整体协调、管理维护和可持续发展的原则，节地、节能、节水、减污，改善居住地域的生态环境，满足现代生活的需求。

住宅区市政设施规划考虑的主要内容是各类市政设施的配置，各类市政设施的布局和用地安排，各类市政管线的综合规划。

（1）供水系统

住宅区的供水包括居民生活用水、各类公共服务设施用水、绿化

supply facilities for public services, green water supply, clean water supply and fire water supply.

The water supply system of residential areas is generally consisted of classification water supply system, differential pressure water supply system and quality differentiating water supply system, which should be employed according to the specific needs and conditions. Classification water supply refers to two systems of water supply, domestic water supply (including residents' living water and water for various public services and facilities) and other water supply. Pressure water supply refers to separate water supply for high-rise buildings and multi-level or low-rise buildings. Quality differentiating water supply refers to the water supply of differenting three types of water, high-quality drinking water, general drinking water and low-quality drinking water or that of differenting water for drinking and water for other use. The utilization of different combination of water supply systems according to different needs aims at reducing long-term operating costs to save energy and water resources.

(2) Drainage system

The drainage system includes sewage and stormwater drainage systems. In residential areas, domestic sewage is the main sewage discharge.

3.2.4 Outdoor Environmental Landscape

Outdoor environmental landscape in residential areas includes two categories——soft and hard landscapes. The soft landscape takes plant configuration and planting layout as the main content, while the hard landscape mainly refers to the design of walking environment, including vertical floor, ground pavement, marginal effect platform, steps and ramp, embankment and fence, and so on. The major goal of the design of residential outdoor environmental landscape is to create an ecological, pleasant

用水、环境清洁用水和消防水。

住宅区的供水系统一般由分类供水系统、分压供水系统和分质供水系统三种，宜根据需要和具体条件采用。分类供水指生活用水（包括居民生活用水和各类公共服务设施用水）与其他用水（分两个系统供水）；分压供水指高层建筑与多层、低层建筑分压供水；分质供水指优质饮用水、普通饮用水和低质水分三种水质进行供水或饮用水和其他用水分两种水质进行供水。根据不同需要采用不同的供水系统组合，目的在于减少长期的运营成本，节约能源和水资源。

（2）排水系统

排水系统包括污水排水系统和雨水排水系统。对住宅区而言，污水排放主要是指生活污水的排放。

3.2.4 户外环境景观

住宅区的户外环境景观包括软质景观和硬质景观两大类。其中，软质景观以植物配置与种植布局为主要内容，硬质景观主要指步行环境的设计，包括地坪竖向、地面铺装、边缘台地、踏步与坡道、堤岸与围栏等。住宅区户外环境景观设计的主要目标是营造生态化、景观化、宜人化、舒适化的物质环境以及和睦、亲近、

and comfortable material environment and a harmonious, intimate and energetic social and cultural environment.

In outdoor environment landscape design in residential areas, green space is an important part of outdoor environment. The elements of green space generally contain land for plant cultivation (including grass, flowers, shrubs, trees, etc.), sites for pavement which belongs to field for plant cultivation (including foot path, open square for pedestrians, etc.), a movable or fixed water body for plant cultivation. According to the gradation of green space, it is divided into public green space, residential green space between houses, road green space, green space for special purpose etc.

The public green land is the space for the enjoyment of all residents, including the residential area parks, green space in the residential quarters, various outdoor grounds, green land of the residential group and green space of larger houses.

Residential green space between houses refers to the field around houses used for plant cultivation but not belonging to the public residential green space.

Road green space refers to the green space within the boundary of the land, used for building roads, such as flower beds, street trees and grass, etc.

Green space for special purpose refers to the space in which all types of facilities (such as public service facilities, municipal facilities, etc.) are within the boundaries of their respective place.

In the planning and design of residential areas, the use of different types of green space has quite different roles. Public green space and green space for special purpose have function, of accommodating games, sports, walking, fitness and leisure; green road space has more sense of a landscape; the role of residential green space between houses or roads mainly lies in the aspects of ecology and scenery.

具有活力的社会文化环境。

在住宅区户外环境景观设计中，绿地是构成住宅区户外环境的重要组成部分。就绿地的构成要素而言，一般包含有植物种植的用地（包括草皮、花卉、灌木、乔木等）、包含在植物种植用地中的铺装硬地（包含步行道、步行休憩广场等）、可活动的或处于植物种植用地内的水体。就绿地的使用层次而言，又分为公共绿地、宅间宅旁绿地、道路绿地和专用绿地等。

其中，公共绿地指住宅区全体居民共同享受的绿地，包括居住区公园、居住小区集中绿地、各类户外场地、居住组团绿地、较大的住宅院落绿地。

住宅区的宅间宅旁绿地是指位于住宅周围，用于种植绿色植物并不属于住宅区公共绿地的用地；

道路绿地是指在道路用地界线以内的绿地，如花坛、行道树、草皮等；

专用绿地常指各类设施（如公共服务设施、市政设施等）地界内所属绿地。

在住宅区规划设计中，由于各类绿地的使用不同，其作用也不完全一样，其中，具有使用功能的主要是公共绿地和专用绿地，容纳游戏、运动、散步、健身和休闲等；道路绿地则更多的是具有景观性；宅间宅旁绿地的作用主要在于生态和景观方面。

3.2.5 Humanization Design

The landscape design of residential areas should be humane and take all the needs of people as the fundamental starting point, and consider man's scale and activities under the premise of developers' scientific and rational operation, the overall environmental protection and sustainable development in pursuit of a graceful, relaxing, ecological and secure landscape with a strong sense of belonging. For example, modern communities often have pools, then it comes that how to make waterscape without water in winter function as beautiful landscape. For example, the laying of gravels on the bottom of shallow water forms a natural bulkhead, which has an outlook of dry creek during anhydrous period. Some larger hard bottom pool can be used as roller-skating rink or a dance hall to perform a sports entertainment function.

Nowdays, the community during the day is the world of the elderly and children. Especially China will soon enter the ageing society. As a result, how to provide services for the elderly is also what we should seriously concern about. The elderly like to get together to do taijiquan and qigong exercises, play chess or cards, carry children for a walk and chat as leisure activities. For all these requirements of such behaviour patterns, designers should have a careful study. In contrast, the young people go to work during the day, who leave home early in the morning and come back late in the evening. After a busy day in the city, what they need first of all is to relax when they go home. Then how to attain this realm in our design of the community space is also an important part to make the residential area landscape design more humane. At present, in some communities, flower racks are designed large but impractical, because there are no climbers in the lower part and the fundamental role and function of flower racks can not be manifested by only making them become mere ornaments. Some of accesses to houses or main

3.2.5 人性化设计

住宅小区景观设计要做到人性化，就要一切以人的需求为根本出发点，应该在开发商商业运作的科学性及合理性、整体自然环境保护和可持续发展的前提下，以人的尺度、人的活动为出发点，追求一种优雅、放松、生态、安全并有强烈归属感的景观风貌，比如，现在社区内经常有水池，如何使水景在冬季无水的情况下也能成为一种有功能的优美景观。如在浅水池底铺设卵石，形成自然驳岸，在无水期间，呈旱溪风貌，面积稍大的硬底水池在冬季作为旱冰场或舞场，发挥体育娱乐功能。

现在社区内白天大部分是老人和儿童的天下，尤其是中国即将步入老龄化社会，如何为老人服务也是我们要认真关注的问题。老人休闲喜欢聚集打拳练功，围桌下棋打牌，携幼儿散步聊天，对于这些要求的行为模式，设计师都应给予认真研究，而青年人白天上班，早出晚归，在繁忙的城市中奔波，一回到家中需要的首先是放松，如何在社区的空间中通过我们的设计达到这种境界，也是住宅小区景观设计更加人性化的重要一环。现在有的社区内，花架设计大而无当，下部没有攀缘植物，花架的根本作用和功能无法体现而成为一种摆设。有的住宅入户路或主要散步道是凹凸不平的汀步，无法满足轮椅和童车的通行要求，还很容易使老人

walkways are rugged haugh, which can not meet the requirements of wheelchairs and child's vehicles and are very easy to tumble the elderly. As for the detail designs of comfortable rest chairs, stone tables and stools, it needs us to make a careful study from the starting point of human needs.

3.2.6 Ecological Design

Ecologization is to protect and use local natural conditions, save energy and clean up the environment. China is a relatively poor country in water storage, so it is a traditional culture that people live in a habitat near water since ancient times. Where there is water, there will gather people. This is the most importment reason that most residential areas hope to have waterscapes. However, this demand conflicts with China's present situation of lack of water, so an effective solution to this problem is to change water sources.

For example, the rainfall is heavier and more concentrated during summer time, and completely discharged into urban sewer. As a matter of fact, it is not only wasted, but also brings great pressure to the city drainage system temporarily. In contrast, in some developed countries, most of the ground surfacing materials are permeable materials, which not only absorb water on the ground bringing convenience to people's travel, but also accumulate rainwater for use. In northern regions, it is entirely possible to set up water tanks in residential areas. Rainwater, collected by ground water drainage systems, can be used for a waterscape and plant irrigation, which greatly eases the pressure of urban water resources.

Obviously, it will increase a part of investment at early stage of the engineering coustruction. However, considering from the macro-perspective, it is worthwhile because of saving water for the society, less property

跌跤。至于休息座椅的舒适宜人、石桌石凳的围合尺度等细节设计，就更需要我们从人性化需求为出发点去仔细研究。

3.2.6 生态化设计

生态化是指更好地保护和利用当地的自然条件、节约能源、净化环境。生态化设计首先就要解决水源缺乏和审美需求之间的关系问题。我国是一个水资源相对贫乏的国家，而自古以来择水而居是中国传统人居文化的重要特点，有水的地方就能聚人，所以这也是大部分住宅区都希望有水景的重要原因。但这种需求同中国缺水的现状形成矛盾，有效解决这个问题就需要改变水的来源问题。

比如北京地区夏季降雨量较大，时间也比较集中，而现在这部分雨水完全排入城市下水道，不仅没有利用，还给城市排水系统带来巨大的瞬时压力。而在一些发达国家地面铺装材料透水材料，不仅地面不形成积水，给人们出行带来方便，而且可以汇集雨水加以利用。在北方地区，完全可以在住宅区内标高相对较低处设置水箱，通过地面排水系统收集雨水，流入水箱贮存，可以做为水景用水及绿化浇灌使用，大大缓解城市水源压力。

这种做法会给前期工程建设增加部分投资，但是从宏观角度考虑却是非常值得的，因为蓄水不仅为社会节约了水资源，而且小区业主也可降低物业费；对开发商而言，

fees for the escate owners, and an ecological community as a selling point for the developer. It is necessary for the government, developers and design organizations to make efforts to carry out water recycling together, though it needs more investment at early stage and a futher study in technology, as long as it is beneficial to the society. In addition, the government's efforts in carrying out this policy should be increased, which will become key driving force to promote ecology design. The use of reclaimed water is the best example.

Another important aspect of ecology of landscape design is the cultivation of green plants. At present, there're two main deficiencies in the landscape cultivation design developed in China. First, the lack of gradations in the planting design, which results from the limitation of the designer's knowlege and experience. Second, the lack of vegetation quantity, which is mainly due to designer's inadequate knowlege of short-term and long-term effects of the plants, or perhaps because some unit in charge of construction cannot fully express the designer's design concept with scamp work and stint material.

A good cultivation design can not only make the community green and vigorous with flowers in spring and fruit in autumn, but also play an excellent role of purifying air, isolating noise, shielding landscape and softening space, etc. This is also one of the goals of long-term objectives in ecological landscape design of residential areas.

小区定位为生态社区也是一个卖点。虽然前期会增加一些投入，从技术上也需要进一步研究，但是后期社会效益巨大，需要政府、开发商、设计机构各方共同努力推行。另外，政府对这方面的政策力度应该有所加大，也是此项工作能够推进的关键动力，中水的使用就是一个最好的范例。

景观设计生态化的另外一个重要方面是绿色植物的种植问题。目前中国开发的社区中景观种植设计有两个大的不足之处，一是种植设计缺乏层次，这主要是因为设计师的水平限制；二是小区内绿量不够，这主要是因为设计师对于植物材料的近、远期效果认识不足，对所掌握的植物材料的知识和范围不够，也可能由于某些甲方自作主张或施工单位偷工减料，使设计师的设计意图不能完整表达。

好的种植设计不仅能使社区绿色葱茏，春季有花，秋季有果，色彩斑斓而丰富宜人，而且能在净化空气、隔绝噪声、屏蔽景观、柔化空间等方面都起到极好的作用，这也是住宅区景观设计在生态化方面需要长期努力的目标之一。

Chapter 4
Business Quarter Design

第4章
商业区整体规划例讲

Generally in business disfrict design,we always start with an overall overview when we make cases introduction, project report or design explanation. Then we introduce the surrounding environment, characteristics and facilities. Special termns here are basically fixed We will take a virtual businrss district of Beijing (ABC) as an example to introduce business quarter design planning process.

4.1 Building Overview

ABC, one of the top-ten construction projects in the Central Business District (hereinafter referred to CBD) of Beijing, is located on the east of Chang-an Street in Beijing—the First Thoroughtfare of China.Composed of four independent high buildings, it is an comprehensive building of Super-Grade 5A intelligent office with relevant business and service facilities.

ABC is sited on the southwest corner of the Golden Cross Center in the core area of Beijing CBD at the bustling section of the most dignified East Chang-an Street.Within this place numerous large-sized international companies, five-star hotela, foreign embassies, luxury entertainment and shopping mails have gathered, Lying at the focal point of the checkerboard traffic inside CBD, ABC enjoys an extremely convenient traffic. It will become one of the landmark masions inside the CBD core, East Chang-an street and Beijing after completion. The main structure is designed to be dignified, elegant, concise and the internal structure environment friendly, tasteful and liberal. The entire

一般商业区规划案例中，在做案例介绍、项目汇报或设计说明时，我们都会先进行整体的特点概述，然后再介绍周边环境、细节上的设计特色、配套设施等一系列内容；项目规划介绍中有很多的专业术语基本上都是固定的。下面，我们虚拟一个北京的商业区（ABC）的规划案例来进行整个商业区规划流程的学习。

4.1 建筑概述

ABC位于中国北京第一大道东长安街，是北京中央商务CBD十大重点工程项目之一。ABC由四栋独立的高层建筑组成，是以超5A智能型办公为主，配以相应的商业及服务设施的综合性建筑群。

ABC地处北京最为尊贵的东长安街繁华地段，位于CBD核心区"金十字"中心西南角。这里云集了国际大型公司、五星级酒店、外国使馆、高档消费及娱乐场所，交通极为便利，是CBD内网格状交通的焦点。ABC建筑空间设计使其成为城市整体建筑不可分割的重要组成部分，建成后将成为CBD核心区乃至整个北京市的标志性建筑物之一。建筑本体设计庄重挺拔、简洁优雅；内部构造环保、清新、自由，整体

style embodies the concept of people-orentation and creates a unique office space of high efficiency, health and comfort.

4.2 Environment

4.2.1 Location

With its prime location on the southwest corner of the Golden Cross in the CBD core area and on the east of Chang-an Street in Beijing—the First Thoroughrare of China—ABC faces East Chang-an Streeton the north,borders on the largest city oasis and recreation area-Culture & Art Square of CBD on the south, which links directly to Tonghui River, adjoins Yintai Center on the east and stands next to the Axial road and central green belt of ABC on the west. Therefore it is an irreproducible prime section in Beijing.

4.2.2 Traffic

Almost every nation in the world prides itself in its National Mall, which symbolizes the keel of the capital city, carries the glory, demonstates the digity of a nation and concentrates the political, economic and cultural quintessence of a nation. In the endless flow of time, the growth and extension of the National Mall is a witness to the development and change of a nation and its people. In WashingtonD.C of the US, the National Mall is a symbol of the coutry's politics and culture; in Paris of France, Champs-Elysees Avenue embodies the stateliness with the State Parliament as well as the charm of Milar. It is same in Moscow, Rome and New Deli. There is a "National Mall", as a "landscape line"for tourists' sight-seeing and a symbol and grandeur of the state machine.

Chang-an Street in China's capital city of Beijing is the "National Mall"in the hearts of the 1.3 billon Chinese people. As the First thoroughfare of the

风格体现以人为本，造就独特高效、健康舒适的办公空间。

4.2 建筑环境

4.2.1 位置

ABC位于中国首都北京神州第一大道——长安街东段，CBD核心区金十字中心西南角的黄金地段。北临东长安街；南临CBD最大的城市绿洲、休闲场所——文化艺术广场，直达通惠河；东临银泰中心；西临CBD中轴线及中心绿化带，是北京不可复制的黄金地段。

4.2.2 交通

几乎世界上每一个国家都有自己的国家大道，每一个国家的国家大道都象征着首都城市的龙骨，承载着一个国家的荣耀，昭示着国家的地位，浓缩着国家政治、经济、文化的精髓。在时间的长河中，国家大道的生长和延伸，就是一个国家、一个民族发展和变化的见证。在美国的华盛顿，国家大道是美国政治、文化的象征；在法国巴黎，香榭丽舍大街既有着国家议会这样威严的法律殿堂，还有着艺术浪漫之都的米兰风情；在俄罗斯的莫斯科，在意大利的罗马，在印度的新德里……在许多国家的首都，都有这样一条既是旅游者漫步观光的"风景线"，又是呈现国家机器庄严的"国家大道"。

在中国首都北京，长安街就是13亿中国人民心中的"国家大道"。作为"神州第一大道"，长

Divine Land, Chang-an Street is the site of many state political and administrative organs, important economic and financial institutions and well-known large-sized public buildings. The Tian An Men Rostrum and Square, symbol of the People's Republic of China, is located near Chang-an Street and in the minds of all the people in China, reflecting the image of the capital and the nation. All of the international and domestic large enterprises long for a place on Chang-an Street in order to demonsrate their enterprise image and strength. ABC just stands tall and upright on the eastern part of this National Mall.

4.3 Architectural Design Concept

4.3.1 Location in Details

It is right opposite to the seven-storey high west wing of the China World Trade Center and a large plot of green land. On the south it borders on the largest green space inside CBD-Culture & Art Square and a sightseeing waterscape on the eastside of Beijing-Tonghui River. It can not only scan widely due to the open space from the south to the north, but also appreciate the green space and running water. This is a fantastic office location in the hustle and bustle metropolitan. In addition, the traffic is very convenient. It is encircled by Chang-an Street, CBD Axial Road, Third Ring Road, Culture & Art Square and Tonghui River North Road, so that it becomes the focal point of the checkerboard shaped traffic inside the CBD. There is easy access to it from any direction and by any mean.

With respect to the architectural space design concept, the investor and designer have taken into full consideration of organic integration and rational utilization of the city, street, pedestrian and green lands, making ABC an indivisible component of the entire building complexes of the city.ABC is a classic of architectural design with its dignified,

安街上分布着众多的国家党政机关、重要的经济金融机构和知名的大型公共建筑，中华人民共和国的象征——天安门城楼和广场就坐落在中间。长安街在我国政治生活和全国人民心目中具有特殊的意义和神圣的地位，体现着首都形象和国家形象，国际、国内大型企业都希望在长安街上立有一席之地，以展示企业的形象及实力。而ABC就耸立在这条国家大道的东段。

4.3 建筑设计理念

4.3.1 项目区位

该项目正对面是仅七层的国贸西楼和大片绿地，南临CBD内最大的集中绿地——文化艺术广场和北京东部观光水景——通惠河，不仅因南北空阔而放眼怡畅，且能欣赏到青青绿地和潺潺流水。这在拥挤、繁华的大都市是不可多得的绝佳办公场所。ABC交通极为便利，长安街、ABC中轴路、三环路、文化艺术广场、通惠河北路将ABC中心环绕其中，使其成为ABC内网格状交通的枢纽地段，无论从任何方向、采取任何方式都可以快捷到达。

在建筑空间的设计理念上，投资人和设计师均充分考虑城市、街道、行人、绿地的有机组合和合理利用，使得ABC成为城市整体建筑群中不可分割的重要部分，并以稳重、挺拔、优雅、间接的本体设计，造就建筑设计的经典，

erect, elegant and concise main body design and an important modern environment friendly culture landscape embodying the humanization of Chang-an Street in the CBD core area.

4.3.2 Design Concept

The design not only focuses on maintaining the overall unity with urban space, but also stress the tune with regional environment in the city. At the same time, it integrates urban space with urban transportation, making the buildings become an integral part of the city. Therefore, ABC and the city can complement, interact and interrelat each other, while ABC itself is able to stand on its own. With its unique architectural style of urban design achievements, outdoor design reflects simple and noble, prudent, tall and straight; in-door design of the main features focuses on the environmental protection, comfort, clean air quality no sense of repression.

4.3.3 Materialization of Design Concepts

ABC has a good sight, for there are no high buildings to both south and north sides of the building. The buildings in the CBD blueprint assume the horizon line shape, transitioning gradually from the height of 300 m from the core area to that of 60 m on the periphery. The height of the business buildings in the core area is generally over 100m, that of the mixed area surrounding the business area generally below 100m and that of the residential area between 60m to 80m.

On the northeast side of ABC area lie the built-up China World Hotel and the Phase 1&2 of the China World Trade Center. The west wing of the China World Trade Center is no more than 30 m, which lies in the other side of Chang-an street to the north of ABC. The axial road of CBD is lying in the west of ABC with a wide central green belt of 20m. With the Beijing Yintai Center in the east and Culture &Art Square, Tonghui River in the south, ABC face no buildings in the south in a radiation

成为体现长安街、CBD核心区人性化的重要现代环保人文景观。

4.3.2 设计理念

该设计不仅从形态上注重保持和城市空间的整体统一，更强调和城市区域环境的协调。同时，在近地空间上和城市交通进行有效的接轨，将建筑融为城市不可分割的部分，使之既相互补充，相互作用，相互关联，又能够独立存在。该区域以其独特的设计成就城市建筑风格。外观设计体现高贵简洁、稳重、挺拔；内部功能设计主要体现环保、舒适、空气清新、不压抑的品质。

4.3.3 设计理念的实现

建筑南北两向无高大建筑，视野宽阔。CBD规划的建筑呈天际线形态，从核心区建筑高度300多米到周边的建筑高60多米逐步过渡，核心区建筑高度一般在100米以上，商务区周边的混合区一般在100米以下，居住区在60至80米之间。

ABC东北侧已建成的中国大饭店及国贸中心一、二期。北临长安街，对侧为国贸西楼及绿地，楼高不到30米；西临CBD中轴路，加20米宽的CBD中心绿化带；东为在建中的北京银泰中心；正南侧为绿地——文化艺术广场和通惠河；整个南面在800米范围内没有任何其他建筑物；东南侧

of 800 m. Jianguomenwai integrated SOHO residential area under construction is situated on southeast side and southwest side.

ABC is situated in the core of CBD, whose front looks down on the buildings across the broad chang-an street. It faces the flat and broad Culture & Art Square of the CBD central green belt on the south. People inside the Center are capable of enjoying wide visual field on both the southern and northern sides and breathe freely and easily without any sense of repression.This is what you may call "looking far without going high".

4.4 Conceptual Design

4.4.1 Design Principles

Core design principles:

Humanization.

Overall sense.

Freedom.

Privacy.

Practicality.

Emphasis of environmental protection

4.4.2 Design Outline and Details

The floor area ratio of ABC is only 5.7, which is rare in such a hustle and bustle metropolis. The storey height of a standard floor inside the building is 4 m. The developer sacrifices the area for a cosy space for user. A 3 m healthy and comfortable net height is possible after a suspended ceiling is installed in the standard floors. The storey height of commercial area is 5.2 m, which is extremely rare in properties of the same level. Such a spacious, comfortable and bright space produces no sense of depression and gives people the space to enjoy the healthy breaths more freely. The minimum utilization efficiency of the standard floors of the four office buildings is >78%, creating a new standard of Grade 5A intelligent office building and achieving the best performance, price ratio

及西南侧为建设中的建外SOHO综合住宅区。

ABC地处CBD核心,建筑正立面间隔宽阔的长安街,一眼望去可对北侧建筑进行俯视,没有任何遮挡,南临CBD中心绿化带平坦宽广的文化艺术广场,该格局使得在建筑物内的人能够在南北两面拥有开阔的视野,通畅自由的呼吸,没有任何压抑感,即所谓临远无须登高。

4.4 方案设计

4.4.1 设计原则

设计原则中的核心体现点:

人性化

整体感

自由度

私密性

实用性

重环保

4.4.2 设计要点与细节

ABC容积率仅为5.7,这在拥挤繁华的大都市是很少见的。楼内标准层层高达4米,标准层吊顶后净高能达3米的健康舒适空间,而这一切都是开发商牺牲面积给您换取的绝无仅有的空间享受。商业空间的层高设计在5.2米,这在同档次的物业中也是非常少见的。在宽敞舒适明亮的空间中,没有压抑感,使人能够更自在地享受,更健康地呼吸。四幢写字楼标准层使用率最低为78%,创造了5A智能型写字楼的新标准,在京城同档次的写字楼中达到最好的性价比;独特的自然通风和

among the office buildings of the same class in Beijing. The unique design of natural ventilation and air conditioning system brings you endless fresh air. Concept of human priority, high quality and accuracy are achieved by humanized toilets, natural ventilation and air conditioning system, reasonable separation of pedestrians and vehicles, application of energy-saving and environment-friendly materials, delicate basement and greenbelts. Design of ABC is aimed at creating a fresh, and free, healthy and elegant, unique and efficient office space for clients.

(1) Function Layout

There are 4 buildings in 3 groups, while 2 super-high-rises in the north and the other 2 in the south are in two groups with office and commercial functions. These buildings are designed in the principle of mutually independent architectural design, due to independent use, convenient management.

In the area between the super-high-rises, entrances and exits to underground parking lots are designed to offer service for these 4 buildings.

(2) Building Function Distribution

Above ground structure

1st to 3rd floors: lobby, public service area and commercial area

4th to 16th floors: standard office floors

17th floor: emergency floor

18th to top floors: standard office floors

Underground structure

B1 & B2 partial: commercial area

B2 & B3: garage equipment room and employees cafeteria

B4: underground civil air defense (garage in normal time)

(3) Profile Design

Semi-ellipse shape is adopted as the basic profile of the buildings, whose roofs are high in the north and low in the south to match with

空调系统设计，不断送来清新的空气；人性化的洗手间、仔细周到的竖向交通组织、合理的人车分流、节能环保材料的运用及消防、地下室、绿化等等设计，对每一个细节近乎苛刻的要求，体现着投资者以人为本、注重品质、精益求精的设计理念，力求为入驻者创造清新自在、健康优雅、独特高效的办公空间。

（1）功能分布

地上建筑共分4栋3组，北侧2栋1组、南侧2栋2组均为超高层建筑，功能为办公、商业。在设计上，考虑各楼独立使用，方便管理，建筑设计相对独立。

超高层建筑间设计地下车库出入口两组，为四栋超高层建筑服务。

（2）建筑功能分布

地上建筑

首至三层：大堂及公共服务区、商业区

四至十六层：标准办公层

十七层：避难层

十八至屋顶层：标准办公层

地下建筑

地下一层，局部二层：商业区

地下二至三层：车库、设备机房、职工食堂

地下四层：人防地下室（平时车库）

（3）造型设计

采用半椭圆形作为建筑的基本外轮廓，顶部采用北高南低的方式，以取得与周边环境及南侧

the surrounding and green area in the south. Transparent glass curtain walls and the tall and straight vertical lines are used to strengthen the sense of mightiness of the building. Multi-layer sightseeing balconies are built on the top of the buildings in a gradual retreating mode, which make the roof into another wonder of the building as a fifth elevation together with the roof greening three dimensional nettled grids and open-style glass roof.

(4) Utilization Efficiency

The utilization efficiency of houses refers to the ratio between floorage and building area and it is an important index to measure the utilization efficiency of a property. The house properties in domestic market are normally sold in building area. However, it is the floorage that really matters to clients. The smaller the difference between the two, the higher the utilization efficiency and the more costeffective.

The utilization efficiency decreases along with the increase of floor height, the number of counterpart facilities and the area occupied by the core tube. The utilization efficiency of some super-high intelligent buildings overseas is mostly around 60% and that of the intelligent office buildings of the same class built or under construction in Beijing is from 65% to 70%.

(5) Storey Height

The storey height of a building mainly satisfies the physiological and psychological needs of the people. The net height of office floors is 2.9m, where dients can enjoy the bright and wide space and free breathing.

Physiologically, the bigger the storey height is, the more sunlight and fresh air people can enjoy, and the weaker the sense of depression becomes. In addition, the enlarged space will increase the content of oxygen in the air. Since the polluted air rises with the warm air, it normally stays at

绿地的协调。通透的玻璃幕墙、挺拔的竖线条更强化了建筑的体量感。建筑顶部采用逐级退台的方式提供多层的观景平台，结合屋顶绿化、空间网状梁格、开放式玻璃屋面板，使作为第五立面的屋顶成为建筑的又一精彩之处。

（4）使用率

房屋使用率指使用面积与建筑面积的比例，是衡量物业使用效率的重要标准。目前国内建筑市场上的房产一般都以建筑面积出售，但对客户来说最具有实际使用意义的是使用面积。使用率越高，则使用面积和建筑面积在数值上差距越小，对使用者来说也越划算。

楼层越高，配套设施越多，核心筒所占面积越大，使用率就越低。国外一些超高层智能建筑使用率大多在60%左右，国内目前建成及在建的同档次智能型写字楼使用率平均在65%左右，最高能达70%左右。

（5）层高

建筑的层高主要满足人们的生理需要和心理需要。办公楼楼层净高2.9米，明亮宽敞的空间，可享受更自在的呼吸。

从生理上来讲，层高越高，能够享受到的光线、清新空气就越多。空间的加大使得空气中的氧气含量增高；由于受污染的空气往往是随着热空气上升，一般集中停滞在层高的大约2/3的上部

the upper space, which is about 2/3 of the storey height. If the storey height is too low, the polluted air will stay at the upper part of the office space and prevents the people indoors from breathing fresh air.

Psychologically, the wide open office space was brought about by giving people a sense of static, delay the pace of life, ease the tension of psychological pressure, and increase work efficiency.

ABC learns experiences of foreign CBD and the construction of the all-around with full respect for the feelings of users, taking an unprecedented clear height of 2.9 meters. It gives you a more spacious and comfortable office space.

(6) Opening Windows and Curtains Design

Unique opening of window curtain wall design will help you enjoy cleaner air and breathe much easier.

Considering the particular geotraphical location of Beijing, spring and autumn are transitional seasons with little difference in temperature, so natural ventilation will be applied, instead of central air conditioning system to adjust indoor temperature and air quality. As a result, the project can be cost-effective and environment friendly. Operable windows are installed on every window, which cover 1/4 the area of effective curtain (1/8—1/12 in other project), so that indoor air is ensured to be circulated and fresh. All the openable windows can be opened with downward-rotation, which is the most advanced technique in the world. That is to say, windows can be opened towards inside near the ground, which can take fresh air easily to heads of people, and help people breathe more comfortable.

(7) Material Selection and Decoration

Material selection should be based on the rank and quality of the building . Designers

空间，如果层高过低，污染的空气往往会停留在供人呼吸的主要空间，使室内的人无法呼吸到新鲜空气。

从心理上来说，层高越高，光线越充足，空间的压抑感就越弱，同时，开阔宽大的办公空间给人心里带来静态感，可以延缓生活节奏，缓解紧张的心理压力，提高工作效率。

ABC借鉴国外CBD及周边建筑的经验，充分尊重使用者的感受，采用前所未有的2.9米的净高，给使用者更为宽敞自由的办公空间，舒适惬意的人性化办公环境。

（6）开启窗幕墙设计

独特的开启窗幕墙设计，使空气更清新，呼吸更顺畅。

考虑到北京地域的特殊性，春秋为过渡季节，温差不大，可直接采用自然通风，不需使用中央空调系统调节室内温度及空气质量，既节省开支，又环保。每一组玻璃均设计有可开启窗，可开启窗占有效幕墙面积的1/4（一般为1/8~1/12），保证室内空气的流通清新。可开启窗采用目前世界上最先进的下旋式开启方式，即在靠近地面位置向内开启，使得新鲜空气自下而上更容易到达人的头部，使人的呼吸更舒适、顺畅。

（7）材料选择及装修

材料选择要与建筑自身的定位、品质相匹配，力求做到简洁、

should try their best to build the construction to be high-graded, clean, graceful, solid and easily maintainable. The materials selected for major parts are as follows:

Exterior decoration Podium: dry laid natural granite connected with the double-layer hollow LOW-E from ribbed points to glass curtain wall.

Main body: vertical dry laid natural granite wall surface, double layer hollow LOW-E transparent glass curtain wall and erected support of aluminum alloy. The best-quality insulated section bars with low heat transfer factor are used for curtain wall frame and bars.

Roof: aluminum alloy weather plate.

Interior decoration: fine decoration shall be completed with the public area and preliminary decoration with the rest part. Natural marbles are used to pave the floors and walls of the lobby on the 1st floor and elevator hoist way (except for the equipment floor and vigil air defense floor). Superior ceramic tiles are used to pave the floors and walls of the middle section washroom on each floor. The office areas are paved by Koehler bricks from Germany on the floors, with no suspended ceilings or with mineral wool sound absorbing plate ceilings according to their own requirement. The walls can be completed to the structural layer in the commercial a service areas.

Granite can be used on the solid exterior walls, which is steady, durable with pleasant bright and graceful looking.

(8) Intelligent System

Building automatic control system: A group of equipment is operated separately and controlled by central operation station, which provides a ideal environment with good air condition. It also supplies a safe, efficient and energy saving office with equipments for emergency prevention and high efficiency transportation, which will help client reduce cost and labor of energy and

大方、牢固、易维护等。主要部位材料选择如下：

裙房部分：石材（天然花岗岩）+双层中空LOW-E玻璃，肋式点连接玻璃幕墙。

主体部分：竖向花岗岩石材墙面+双层中空LOE-E高通透玻璃+铝合金，使用传热系数较低的断热型材做幕墙杆件和框料。

屋顶部分：铝合金封檐板。

内部装修：公用空间精装修完成，其余部分初装完成。首层大堂、各层电梯间（设备层及人防层除外）地面、墙面均采用天然大理石铺设；各层中筒部位的卫生间地面、墙面铺设高级瓷砖，办公区域地面全部铺设网络地板，一般不吊顶，也可根据自身要求局部做矿棉吸音板吊顶。商业及服务区域只做到结构面。

外部实体部分：使用花岗岩，稳重、耐久、美观亮丽、优雅。

（8）智能化系统

楼宇自动控制系统通过中央操作站集中管理、分散控制，为使用者提供舒适——良好的空气环境，节能——降低能耗和管理成本，安全——提供突发故障的预防手段，高效——提高设备运行效率减少管理人员的数量，充分的可扩展性——保证日后发展

management. Enough expansibility can ensure enough space for the development in the future.

Integrated wiring and communication system: Six-class non-shielding cable system is applied, which can support 1 KM Ethernet transmission. This configuration can completely satisfy the demands of commercial units, such as bank, securities, broadcast and media companies, which have a high requirement of internet quality and speed. The standard offices are paved with the intelligent network floor, which is conveniently configured and helps devices reach the information points directively in accordance with their own requirements. Integrated wiring system can realize resource sharing in the global scale, comprehensive data and information management, email, personal database, report and financial management, audio & video conference.

Fire automatic alarm and fire-fighting linkage control system are figured with the special Grade A protection.

Safeguard monitoring system.

Community Cable TV television and satellite TV receiving system.

Background music and emergency broadcasting system

Parking lot intelligent management system.

Wireless communication covering system to make sure wireless communications without blind spots in building.

(9) Air-conditioning Fresh Air System

The air-conditioning main frame system is 100% imported well-known international brand, and te terminal syatem is air blower coil pipe and fresh air system. The air blowing volume is 80% of the fresh air.

Indoor design parameter:

Indoor designed temperature in summer: 24℃ ; Relative humidity: 60%.

Indoor designed temperature in winter: 22℃ ;

所需的足够空间。

综合布线及交通系统采用目前六类非屏蔽线缆布线，可支持千兆以太网的传输。该配置完全能满足像银行、证券公司、传播媒体公司等对网络质量及速度要求较高的行业从事经营活动。标准办公区域采用智能化，方便配置的网络地板铺设，该设施可根据自身需求直达信息点。综合布线系统可以快速实现世界范围资源共享、综合信息数据管理、电子邮件、个人数据库、报表处理、财务管理、电话会议、电视会议等。

火灾自动报警及消防联动控制系统，设置特一级保护。

保安监控系统。
有线电视及卫星电视接收系统。

背景音乐及紧急广播系统

停车场智能化管理系统。

无线通讯覆盖系统，保证在楼内无线通讯基本无盲区。

（9）空调新风系统

空调系统末端为风机盘管加新风设计，排风量为新风量的80%。

室内设计参数：
夏季室内设计温度24℃，相对湿度60%。

冬季室内设计温度22℃，相

Relative humidity: 40%.

Fresh air machine is equipped for each floor. The fresh air is transmitted to the fresh air machine in each floor after pressurization by the air blower.

Fresh air volume:

Office area: 30m^3 /h

Underground cafeteria: 20m^3 /h.

Underground commercial area : 15m^3 /h.

The core tube toilet:

The independent mechanical air blowing system for separated section and the air blowing colume is 10 times per hour and the air blowing volume (including the core tube toilet air blowing volume) in each floor is 80% of the fresh air on each floor. The air blowing systems are independent between the toilet and office to ensure the air quality in the office space.

(10) Elevator System——Vertical Transportation in the Building

As for the office elevator of two super-high buildings in the north side, there are two groups of imported elevators (four sets of one group) with famous international brand running in the divided areas from 1st floor to the 18th, and from the 18th to the top floor. The speed of higher area elevator runs at 4m/s. There are two imported guests' elevators respectively in the two super-high buildings in the north side with the main function of vertical transportation from B5 to the roof floor.

As for the office elevator of two super-high buildings in the south side, there are two groups of imported elevators (four sets of one group).

There is an elevator for fire control in each building, which has a transportation from B5 to the top floor. Two groups of anti-fire stairways' with width of 1.2m are set in each of four super-high buildings as accesses from B5 up to the top floor.

Advantages of separating guests' elevator from office elevator:

对湿度40%。

机组设置：新风机组按层设置，新风经风机加压后通过竖井接至各层新风机组。

新风量：

办公区域 30 立方米/小时

地下餐厅 20 立方米/小时

地下商业 15 立方米/小时

卫生间排风系统：

核心筒卫生间分段设置独立的机械排风系统，排风量为 10 次/小时，各层排风量（含核心筒卫生间排风量）为各层新风量的 80%。卫生间排风系统与办公空间的排风系统各自独立，保证了办公空间空气的质量。

（10）电梯系统——楼内竖向交通

北侧两栋设有超高层建筑办公用梯，每栋有两组高速电梯（每组四部）分区进行，运行区间为首层至十八层、十八层至顶层两个分区，电梯运行速度可达 4 米/秒；此外，每栋另设有两部进口客梯，主要功能是负责地下五层至首层的竖向运输。

南侧两栋设有超高层建筑办公用梯，每栋有两组高速电梯（每组四部）分区运行。

南北每栋建筑均设有一部消防电梯，由地下 5 层运行至顶层。四幢超高层建筑每栋分别有两组疏散楼梯，宽度为 1.2 米，可通达地下五层至顶层。

将客梯和办公电梯分开设置的好处在于：

First, it is more convenient to protect the privacy and independence of office by avoiding people go to office directly from underground elevator.

Second, use efficiency of elevator above ground are improved.

(11) Internal Traffic Panning

Principle of the planning: independent entrances and exits, segregation of commercial and office traffic, people and vehicles, and enough space in reserve for transformation in the future.

Motor vehicles: The motor vehicle entrances are set on the eastern and southern sides of the building area. The one on the eastern side mainly serves the 2 super-high-rises in the north area, while the one on the southern side mainly serves the 2 super-high-rises in the south area . Traffic flows will be analysed in details in traffic analysis chart.

People flow: The office people flow to the two northern super-high-rises buildings can directly enter the buildings from the entrance adjacent to the northern sides of Chang-an Street and the southern entrance adjacent to the square; the office people flow to the two southern super-high buildings can enter the buildings directly by road and the southern gate of the buildings. People flow for business can enter the northern super-high-rises by lobby gate or the drownbasin squre to the underground business area.

Parking: Parking lots of motor vehicles are mainly built underground and the parking lots above ground are mainly for the temporary use of visitors. Two entrances are designed on both the eastern and western side of the building area to serve all the super-high buildings.

(12) Power Supply System

Double lines of 10kV power source are independent from each other, while alternative lines are with dual-loop terminals for important positions. Uninterrupted power sources are adopted for important equipment and facilities (such as

第一、方便管理，保证了办公层相对的私密性和独立性，避免从地下电梯直达办公层；

第二、增加地上办公层电梯的使用率。

（11）内部交通规划

规划的出发点：各出入口独立、商业办公分流，人车分流，同时留有足够充分的改造余地。

机动车：机动车入口设置在建筑用地东侧及南侧。东侧机动车入口主要为北侧两栋超高层建筑服务，南侧机动车入口为南侧两栋超高层建筑服务，其交通流线组织将在交通分析图中详细剖析。

人流：进入北侧两栋高楼建筑的办公人流可从临长安街的北侧及临广场的南侧入口直接进入；进入南侧两栋超高层建筑的办公人流可从南侧城市道路及楼群南口直接进入，商业人流可通过北侧两栋超高层的独立门厅和南面下沉式广场直接进入地下商业区。

停车：机动车停车位主要布置在地下，地上车位主要供访客临时使用。建筑用地东西两侧有出入口各一组，为整个超高层建筑服务。

（12）供电系统

用两路独立的10kV电源，重要部位采用双回路末端互投，重要设施设备（如中控室、计算机中心、电梯、报警系统等）设置不间断电源（EPS电源）。两路

central control room, computer centre, elevator and alarm system). The 10kV high-voltage distribution sources shall supply power simultaneously, so that if either one of them sufferes from fault or blackout, the interconnection switch shall automatically close and the alternative line of power source shall bear 80% of the total load.

(13) Water Supply System

Water supply and drainage system:

Domestic water supply system.

Domestic hot water system:

Domestic hot water shall be supplied centrally and prepared by accumulated electric water heater;

Water drainage system.

Intermediate water system (Biological contact oxidization treatment), sewage and rainwater system.

(14) People–Oriented Toilet Design

The width of stools in toilets on each floor of ABC is designed no less than 1m, larger than the standard stool width of 0.9m, which is more convenient than the other buildings of the same grade. Users with larger size will feel more comfortable when using the toilet. Besides the toilets in the core area, water supply and drainage pipes are reserved for VIP toilets with two sets of independent sanitation systems, from which the clients can have the options of either choosing the public sanitary system or setting a separate sanitary system in the private office area. The toilets for men and women are designed in a human-oriented way according to the physiological features of the two sexes. For example there are more urinals' in men's toilet and more lavatories in the women's toilet. Toilets special for the handicapped are installed in the commercial and service spaces from the B1 to the 3rd floor.

(15) Underground Civil Defense Design

Grade 6 civil defense facilities shall be set in the underground 4th and 5th floors, which will be

10kV高压配电电源同时供电，当任何一路发生故障或停电时，供电系统自动互投，另一路电源能承担全部负荷80%。

（13）给排水系统

生活给水系统：

中高区配备变频恒压供水设备；

生活热水系统：

集中生活热水由蓄热式电热水器制备；

排水系统：

分设中水系统（采用生物接触氧化法处理）、污水系统。

（14）卫生间设计

ABC各层的卫生间每个蹲位，设计宽度都在1米以上，超过国家甲级写字楼标准为卫生间宽度0.9米要求，比一般同档次写字楼卫生间的使用更舒服，可以减少身材高大者使用时的压迫感。除每层核心筒内的卫生间外，还预留了设置VIP卫生间的上、下水管道，相当于设计了两条独立的卫生系统，客户既可以选择每层所在的公共卫生系统，也可以选择在所属的办公区域内单独设置私属卫生系统。男、女卫生间分别根据其生理特点人性化设计。如男卫生间小便器多，女卫生间坐便器多。地下1层至地上3层商业及服务设施空间内设计有残疾人卫生间。

（15）地下人防设计

在地下四、五层设置六级人防设施（平时作车库，战时作为

used as a garage in normal time and storage during wars.

(16) Facilities for the Handicapped

All buildings are installed with non-obstacle ramp and entrance, parking lots, toilet and elevator for the handicapped and roads for the blind.

(17) Fire Control Design

Fire protection Grade: Grade A Class A. The buildings are furnished with helicopter platform, emergency floor and other facilities.

Fire-fighting passage, the fire-fighting surface, anti-fire stairways and fire-fighting elevator shall be designed and located in full accordance the relevant state codes. There is an emergency floor on every floor.

(18) Environ mental Protection and Energy Saving

No emission of poisonous or harmful gas or liquid are discarded during and after the project construction. Waste water is discarded after receive intermediate water treatment before entering water drainage systems. OLW-E highly transparent hollow glass is used to improve the quality of the building while avoid warm island effect by high transparency and low heat transfer factor.

(19) Changeable Design.

Considering sustainability and changes caused by the society and the metropolis with era, the design has left sufficient room in the function configuration, office floor height, intelligent arrangement and floor loads. As a result, there is enough space for changes in the future.

(20) Greening Plan for Surrounding Area

The greening system near ABC aims at expanding the open public space at the joint of major roads with the buildings, making the building

库房）。

（16）方便残疾人设施

各楼均按照国家规范设置无障碍坡道及入口、残疾人停车位、盲道、残疾人卫生间及残疾人电梯等设施。

（17）消防设计

消防等级为高层一级一类。设有直升机救援平台、避难层等设施。

消防通道的设计及扑救面的位置完全按照国家相关规范设置。严格按照规范要求设置疏散楼梯及消防电梯，并且各楼均设有避难层。

（18）环保及节能

该项目在建设过程中和建成以后均无有毒、有害气体或液体排出，排水系统作中水处理后进入市政管道，采用LOW-E高通透中空玻璃、断热冷桥幕墙结合局部开放式幕墙构造系统以达到高通透性且传热系数较低的要求，既能保证该建筑物的品质，又避免造成城市"热岛效应"。

（19）可变性设计

考虑到社会及都市不断地随时代的发展而变化，该建筑设计充分考虑其可持续发展性，在功能配置、办公室层高、智能化布置及楼板荷载设计方面都留有足够的空间，为将来功能需求发生变化进行可变式设计提供充足的空间。

（20）规划周边绿化

ABC绿化系统的规划目标是：在主要道路和建筑相交处尽量放大公共开放空间，在增强它的开阔

easily-recognizable and strongly-guiding as a landmark, and providing a leeway for rest. It can supply a space of free breath and a good standpoint to view dense building groups in the CBD in distance.

Closely adjacent to the central axial road of CBD, ABC is designed to have a 20m-wide green belt at street, a green belt of 50m wide to the north of Chang-an street, and a green square of 50,000m^2 in the CBD. Good location and environment give the buildings a high taste and novel spirit.

性、识别性和导向性的同时，为持续、紧张的街道界面提供一个自由呼吸的空间，为CBD密集的建筑群体提供一个观赏的距离。

ABC紧邻CBD中轴路，临街设计有20米宽的绿化带，北侧临长安街一侧设计有50米绿化带，南侧为CBD区域级5万平方米的广场集中绿地。幽雅的周边环境和卓越的地理位置为ABC的品质奠定的基础，使其成为真正的绿色、有氧环抱中的财智至尊建筑。

Chapter 5
Exhibition Design

第5章
展示空间设计

5.1 Concept of Exhibition Design

Exhibition means display, which is to display or demonstrate goods or concept in a static or dynamic form in certain space to achieve the main function of attracting, conveying and communicating.

Exhibition design is a subject of rich content involving a wide range of areas, and constantly enriches its content with the development of times. Exhibition design is an integrated design art. From the perspective of space, it has both the artistic style of building space and the sculpture spirit symbolizing expressionism. From the point of view of graphic design, each dimension of the display shows the charm of visual communication. From the perspective of industrial design, the display case, the display shelf and the booth are refined products for their the shape and functions. From the perspective of the environmental design, the atmosphere of the whole space is like the charming stage. It involves so many aspects that it requires the designer to be an expert familiar with various techniques and materials, who can make use of all kinds of artistic, scientific and technological methods focusing on the display goal to create the best display space.

5.1.1 Development of Modern Exhibition

From the 1861 World Expo in London's Hyde Park, the 1925 Paris Exposition and various world-scale trade fairs to Disneyland, we are surrounded by exhibition everywhere.

5.1 概念

展示即展览，是在一定空间内以动静态的形式将物品或概念陈列演示出来，以达到招引、传达、沟通的主要机能。

展示设计是一个有着丰富内容，涉及广泛领域并随着时代发展而不断充实其内涵的课题。展示设计同时是一门综合的设计艺术：从空间上，既具备建筑空间的艺术风格，又具备象征表现主义的雕塑精神；从平面设计角度方面审视，每个展示面充分显示了视觉传达的魅力；从工业设计角度审视，在从造型和功能上，展柜、展架、展台是精致的产品；从环境设计方面审视，整体空间的氛围营造如同迷人的舞台。涉及的方面如此之多，故要求设计师必须是一个掌握和熟识各种技术和材料的专家，能围绕自己展示的目标调动各种艺术的、科学的、技术的手段，创造最佳的展示空间。

5.1.1 现代展示的发展

从1861年伦敦海德公园的世界博览会、1925年的巴黎博览会以及各种世界规模的交易会，到迪斯尼乐园及各类商品展销会、各种商品陈列等无一不是我们熟悉的例子。

Though these exhibitions are quite different in scale and nature, they still have similar design characteristics. In recent years, many worldwide exhibitions follow the trend of high input and long-term. Some famous museums do not hesitate to invest a large amount of money, labor and material resources with latest scientific and ecological achievements, so that an exhibition becomes an artistic and cultural activity containing both top technology and intensive information

5.1.2 Objective of Exhibition Design

The objective of exhibition design is not to show itself, but to display the contents to the audience purposefully and logically through space planning, layout, lighting control, color scheme and organizations. It tries to make the audience accept the information conveyed in the design. Therefore, exhibition is a special form of commercial advertising.

5.1.3 Significance of Exhibitions

Exhibition is a marketing activity highly concentrated of time and space. Exhibitors can negotiate with hundreds of thousands of customers face-to-face and sign contracts in a short period of time. It also supply exhibitors a chance to understand the similar and related industries comprehensively and adjust their business strategy. A successful exhibition can even ascertain the whole year's sales plan. As a result, business exhibitions and fairs still show great vitality and are highly favored by businessmen in the information era, when the means of information exchange is highly developed.

Modern commercial exhibition is no longer consisted of a table, two chairs and a few boards, which is regarded a passive display like modern "temple fair". In the fierce exhibition competition, it is a key to success of displaying the image of

尽管这些展示在规模和性质上有着很大的差别，但在设计的性质上有着相近特点。近年，世界各国的许多展示都呈现出高投入、长期化的趋势，一些著名的博物馆都不惜巨资，投入大量人力物力，运用最新科技成果，使展示成为一种融尖端科技和密集信息的艺术性的文化活动。

5.1.2 展示设计的目的

从展示设计的角度而言，设计的目的并不是展示本身，而是通过设计，运用空间规划、平面布置、灯光控制、色彩配置以及各种组织策划，有计划、有目的、符合逻辑地将展示的内容展现给观众，并力求使观众接受设计所计划传达的信息，所以说，展示是商业特殊形式的广告。

5.1.3 展示设计的意义

展示会对营销活动的时间与空间进行了高度浓缩：短短几天，可以和成百上千的客户面对面洽谈、签约，全面了解同类及相关行业的发展水平，从而调整自己的经营方略。一次成功的展览会，甚至可以落实全年度的销售计划。正因如此，在信息交流手段高度发达的资讯时代，商业展览会、交易会依然呈现勃勃生机，深得商家青睐。

现代商业展览，早已不再是一桌两椅、几块展板，现代"庙会"式的被动展示。在激烈的展览竞争中，除策划、组织工作外，展示的形象设计也是展览会成功

the exhibition design, in addition to planning and organization. How to break through the limited space constraints and make full use of exhibition features is a problem that an exhibition design must solve.

5.1.4 Relations between Small Themes

In addition to the display of each item, the relationship between small themes is also the focus of discussion. The links between the relationship of small themes and exhibition space style are also closely.

Exhibition design is a complicated artistic creation process involved many subjects. It has an obvious objective, that is, to coordinate the rationality between human being and the provided space in certain circumstances, so that the design result can influence or change human's living state, and brand benefits can be improved in commercial effect. In a word, exhibition design is the demonstration in a static or dynamic form in certain space, which has the main function of attracting, conveying and communicating in order to make a purposeful and premeditated space design of image publicity.

5.1.5 Design Concept Expression

Three elements of the exhibition design: organizer, exhibits and audience.

The attainment of basic aim of exhibition is the source of design concept, that is, the original dynamic force of creation, whether it adapts to the requirements of the design plan and can solve problems. The approach to acquire such concept should base on the scientific and rational analysis to discover problems then make a plan to solve the problem. The whole process is a gradual and natural hatching process. The design concept should be formed as natural as water flows on the basis of information possession, but not like the sudden outburst of personal awareness of art activities. Naturally, in the design process, rational analysis

的关键。如何突破有限的空间限制，最大限度地发挥展览功能，是展示设计必须解决的问题。

5.1.4 小主题的联系

除了每个项目的展示意图外，各小主题间的关系也是讨论的重点，由小主题的关系所构成的联系和展示空间的格调也息息相关。

展示设计是涉及众多学科的一项复杂的艺术创造过程，目的明确，即在一定条件的限制下协调人和空间的合理性，以使其设计结果能够影响和改变人的生活状态，并能在商业效应上获得品牌效益的提升。简言之，在一定空间内，以动静态的陈列布局手段，以招引、传达和沟通为主要机能，进行有目的、有计划的形象宣传的空间设计。

5.1.5 设计理念的表达

展示设计的三个元素：主办者、展品、观众。

展示目的的实现最根本在于设计的概念来源，即原始的创作动力是什么，设计方案是否适应要求。依靠科学和理性的分析以发现问题进而提出解决问题的方案，整个过程是一个循序渐进和自然而然的孵化过程。设计师的设计概念应在他占有相当数量资料的基础上很合理地像流水一样自然流淌出来，而不是像纯艺术活动的突发性个人意识的宣泄。在设计当中，功能的理性分析与艺术形式的完美结合要依靠设计

and perfect combination in art form will be realized depending on the designer's inner virtues and practical experiences. It requires the designer to have a wide range of knowledge, positive attitude and acute observation of life. The complicated analysis process is a hard persevering process which cannot be accomplished by personal efforts. In this case, assistance and team corporation is the key. Though a designer, an engineer or a material planner can cope with the job on his/her own, there will be inevitable loss. Therefore, only well corporate group can complete a perfect design.

5.2 Phases and Focal Points of Exhibition Design

5.2.1 The Early Phase of Exhibition Design

Before starting a design, designers must conceive the general framework of the design. In process of the design and the investigation and knowledge of the data provided by the enterprise, the content of vice themes should be decided at the end of the design. Therefore, exhibition design is affected by contents from the beginning to the end.

5.2.2 Establishment of Framework

This is the key to exhibition design, which decides the direction of design. Design ideas must be based on a theme. In the early stage, designers must first have some knowledge about the message that the company wants to convey to visitors, as the message decides the main theme and style. A good exhibition theme must be able to demonstrate directly the exhibitation contents, and can create a special atmosphere of exhibition, so that the exhibition can attract customers and promote the sale purpose effectively.

5.2.3 Determination of Vice Themes

Vice themes and relative items are complements of the main theme. Each vice theme should become

师内在品质修养与实际经验来实现，这要求设计师应该广泛涉猎不同门类的知识，对任何事物都抱有积极的态度和敏锐的观察。纷繁复杂的分析研究过程是艰苦的坚持过程，一个人的努力是不能完成的，人员的协助与团队协作是关键，单独的设计师、图文工程师或材料师虽然都能独挡一面，却不可避免地会顾此失彼，只有一个配合默契的设计小组才能完成。

5.2 展示设计的各个阶段及重点

5.2.1 展示设计初期阶段

着手设计之初，必须构想展示剧情的大致框架，随着设计作业的进行及对企业提供资料的调查及了解，在基本设计结束时，也要决定展示剧情的各个主题的内容。所以展示设计从始至终受到展示剧情的左右。

5.2.2 建立展示剧情的框架

这是展示设计的关键，它决定着设计的走向。设计构思一定是基于某种主题所成，在基本设计的初期阶段，必须先了解企业要传达给参观者什么信息，由此决定展示的大主题和风格。好的展示主题必须能直接表达展览内容，而且可以创造一种特殊的展览气氛，有效吸引顾客，达到宣传销售目的。

5.2.3 划分小主题

要划分出小主题来补充大主题，还有相关的各种项目，这些

one of the best local points due to their own unique ideas, while subordinating to the overall style.

5.2.4 Coordination of The Overall Style

Wonderful points form the framework of the exhibition story while coordinating with the overall style. Space planning and the modeling arrangement are based on the framework.

5.2.5 Determination of Exhibition Emphases

Mainpoints and zones of exhibition should be established according to the overall style of exhibition theme. Exhibition story will be formed by dividing structure and space with details.

All the business information conveyed in the exhibition design will finally be carried out in various exhibition media such as videos, charts and samples. The distribution of all these exhibition media must be decided in accordance with the contents of the exhibition story.

5.2.6 Use of Innovative Media

Great attention should be paid to the display of important themes. Unexpected effect will be achieved by innovative media. Designers should create all kinds of new media and discuss about the availablility and applicability of these ideas, so that they can not only ensure compliance with the limited exhibition space, but also be of a unified style and can be included in the display story.

5.2.7 Synchronization of the Implementation of Plan and Design

Basic design plan and implementation of the plan will be rewritten with the progress of execution. A final decision will be made during the execution period, such as details and information. However, the design needs modification because of changes in site conditions

内容既要服从整体风格，又要有其独特的构思，能够成为一个个精彩的局域点。

5.2.4 协调整体风格

精彩点必须与整体风格协调起来成为展示剧情的框架，并由此出发考虑场地空间规划及造型结构的安排，开始基本设计。

5.2.5 确立展示重点

根据展示主题和整体风格确立展示重点，划分展示区域和空间及结构关系，规定各种造型细节等，将这些归纳起来，就是展示剧情。

在展览设计中所传达的商业信息，最终要落实到模型、影像、图表、样品等多种展示媒体上。而所有这些展示媒体的分配也必须按照展示剧情的内容来决定。

5.2.6 利用创新媒体

要将重点放在重要主题的展示上，利用创新的媒体来表现展示重点，往往能得到意想不到的效果。利用丰富的想象力来创造各种新颖的宣传媒体，讨论并选择使想法变成可行的具体方案，既保证符合展览场地的限定又具有同主题统一的风格，并纳入展示剧情。

5.2.7 方案与设计实施同步

基本设计方案和实施计划随着设计制作具体作业的进行都要改写。尤其进入设计的实施阶段，设计的细节及在此展开的信息内容都一一有了定案，但有时因为场地条件及信息材料变化的关系，也必须修改

and information materials. As a result, display story is the key to carrying out large exhibition designs.

5.2.8 Commercial Significance of Exhibition

Exhibition is not only art design, but it creates publicizing effect and marketing environment. Its artistic quality is in a lower level than its commercial quality. In a sense, it is the extension and expansion of enterprise products. The amount and quality of business information in a large-scale exhibition display will directly decides the success or failure of exhibitors. Concepts of exhibition story enables designers to grasp all the information completely and accurately, seize market opportunities and establish a good image.

5.3 Subjects of Exhibitions Design

5.3.1 Center of Exhibition Design

Some people consider that exhibition design is object-centered, which is different from human-centered environment art design. However, some people think it is human-centered, otherwise there is no need to take so many human factors and ergonomics into consideration. I disagree with them, while I admit that art is human-centered. I think neither human nor object is the object of exhibition design, but they are both ends linked to the object. The object is the transmission and effective reception of information.

5.3.2 Role of Exhibition

From the perspective of role, no matter a commercial brand promotion, a showcase, or a museum is in purpose of effective information convey. Business practices aims at raising brand awareness and establish reputation, so as to stimulate market. Museums would like to have effective dissemination of culture.

设计。在这种情况下，常常回归的原点就是展示剧情，所以展示剧情是进行大型展示设计时的核心内容。

5.2.8 展示的商业意义

展示设计是创造宣传效果和销售环境而不仅仅是艺术设计，它的艺术性远不及商业性，从某种意义说它是企业商品的扩展延伸，大型展示设计中所注入商业信息的多少，质量的高低，直接影响企业参展的成功与否。构思展示剧情能使设计者完善、准确地把握企业与商品的所有信息，以帮助参展企业抓住市场机遇，树立优良形象。

5.3 展示设计的主体问题

5.3.1 展示设计的中心

有人认为展示设计是以物为中心的设计行为，这区别于以人为中心的环境艺术设计，也有人持相反观点，认为展示设计也是以人为中心的，否则就不需要考虑那么多的人文因素和人体工学。我们的观点与此不同，我们承认环境艺术是以人为中心，同时认为在展示设计中其实人与物都不是主体，而是主体所连接的两头，而这个主体就是信息的传递与有效接收。

5.3.2 展示的作用

从展示的作用来说，不论是商业品牌宣传为目的的展览会、橱窗，还是以文化传播为目的的博物馆，良好的展示空间最重要的功能是有利于信息的有效传递。商业行为是为了提升品牌的认知度和建立口碑，以及刺激购买；博物馆是

Exhibition design is one of the terminal forms of information transmission (advertising, cultural transmission, etc.). When there is an item in a space, then there is a process of information transmission between the item and the visitors. The amount of transmitted information is directly related to the display effect and the arrangement of the display. If there is no item in the display hall, the overall feeling of this space is an abstract object as a brand image, which will give visitors a feeling of a process of information transmission and brand recognition.

5.4 Methods and Procedures of Exhibition Design

5.4.1 Design Planning Stage

The most important of the design is the possession of data, and whether there is a complete investigation and horizontal comparison. After you search for a multitude of data, you summarize and organize the data to find out deficiencies and problems, and then make an analysis. Such a repeated process will make your design gradually distinct when you don't know where to start. Horizontal comparison and investigation of the design patterns of other similar space, the acquirement of the existing problems and experiences, such as its position, traffic conditions, how to use public facilities and how to solve unfavorable problems. You can determine the design orientation according to the range of the audience. You should analyse the staff fluidity and inner work process, and make a reasonable plan. All of these should be solved in the stage of data collection and analysis. In this stage, You should also put forward a reasonable tentative design concept, that is, the overall style orientation of the exhibition space.

为了有效传播文化，展示设计其实是信息传递（广告宣传、文化传播等）的终端实现形式之一。在一个空间内有某一物品，那么这个物品和观者之间就有一种信息传递的过程，信息传递多少，就与展示的效果、布展的方式有直接联系，如果场馆内无物，只是一个提供展示者和参观者交流的空间，那么这个空间的整体感觉就是一个抽象的物，可以被认为是品牌形象，它给参观者的感觉就是信息的传递过程，也是品牌认同或加固的过程。

5.4 展示设计的方法与程序

5.4.1 设计规划阶段

设计的根本首先体现在是否占有充分的资料，是否有完善的调查和横向比较。大量地搜索资料，归纳整理，寻找场地缺陷，发现问题，进而加以分析和补充，这样的反复过程会让你的思路在无所适从中渐渐清晰起来。设计构思阶段要横向比较和调查其他相似空间的设计方式，掌握已存在的问题和经验，例如位置的优劣状况，交通情况，如何利用公共设施，以及如何解决不利矛盾。根据观众的大致范围而确定设计的基本定位，分析人员的流动方向和内部工作流程，合理规划线路。这些在资料收集与分析阶段都应详细地分析与解决。这一阶段还要提出一个合理的初步设计概念，也就是展示空间的大体风格定位。

5.4.2 Overall Analysis Stage

After all these, a perfect and ideal space function analysis drawing should be made, that is a totally and absolutely reasonable function plan abandoning the actual plane. This is to avoid preconceived ideas confining the designer's perceptual thinking, for the original plane is bound to permeate with some design thoughts to some extent in which you will be unconsciously change your ideas.

When you complete the basic plan, then there comes the substantive stage of the design. At this stage, you should conduct a field survey and combine your ideal design with actual space. The exhibition design aimes at narrowing the influence of unfavorable conditions on the field in restricted conditions. You should apply your design ideas to practical field as much as possible, trying to make the field space layout reasonable and contain an overall unity. A reasonable space layout and a good structure will lay a good foundation for the work followed, which benefit the progress of the exhibition centents and help grasp the tempo of the artistic effects.

5.4.3 Developing Stage

During the progress of the conversion from plane to three-dimensional space, the initial design concepts should be improved and carried out in the three-dimensional effect by means of color, lighting and illumination.

The choice of primary materials should submit to an actual problem of budget. A single or complex material is determined by the design concept. Although reducing cost is one principle of the design, luxury materials are still used for demonstrating the ideal design more perfectly. It does not mean that low budget cannot create a reasonable design, but

5.4.2 概要分析阶段

做完设计规划后应提出一个完善的和理想化的空间机能分析图，也就是抛弃实际平面而完全绝对合理的功能规划。这是为了避免因先入为主的观念限制了设计师的感性思维。因为原有的平面渗透着某种程度的设计思想，在无形中会让你改变自己的思路。

当基本构思完成，便进入了实质的设计阶段。这时详细的实地测量以及如何将理想设计与实际空间相结合是这个阶段所要做的。展示设计的目的就是在有限制的条件下通过设计缩小不利条件对场地的影响。将设计构思尽可能多地落实到实际场地中去。使场地空间布局合理，虚实呼应，保持整体的统一性。空间布局合理，结构顺畅，将会为后面的工作打下良好的基础，展示内容的展开，艺术效果的节奏把握都会因之受益。

5.4.3 设计发展阶段

从平面向三维的空间转换，其间要将初期的设计概念完善和实现在三维效果中，其实现手段是材料、色彩、采光和照明。

材料的选择首要的是服从于设计预算这个现实的问题，选择单一或是复杂的材料要因设计概念而确定。虽然低廉的材料要比豪华材料的堆砌更加符合节约成本原则，但有时高品质材料可以更加完美地体现理想设计效果，因此并不是说低预算不能创造合理的设计，也不是

it is better to construct the design by suitable materials. Color, which is complementary to materials, is an indispensable factor to express the design concept. Lighting and illumination are used to create an atmosphere. Although there's some exaggeration in the saying that the art of interior design is the art of lighting, it is a truth that art form is ultimately conveyed to human through visual expression.

The realization of these designs depends on 3D maps to convey themselves to clients, meanwhile the designer improves his design through three-dimensional maps. The performance chart can affect the success of program, but it is not the key factor with assistance. It is very important to remember that the design itself plays a decisive role.

5.4.4 Detail Design Stage

Furniture design, indoor design, lighting design, doors, windows, walls, roof connections and some special expressions of the exhibition contents belong to the improvement stage in the development stage of the design. Most of the problems have been solved in the development stage, this is just to further integrate with the construction and budget .

Construction drawing design is the last procedure of the design work, which can be purely technically performed.

5.5 Function Division and Display Area Arrangement

5.5.1 Basic Principles of Display Space Layout

(1) Dynamic, Sequent and Rhythmical Forms of Display Space

The biggest feature of exhibition space is strong liquidity, so the basic principle to conform

说低预算一定能获得最佳设计，关键是如何选择。色彩是体现设计理念的不可缺少的因素，它和材料是相辅相成的。采光与照明是营造氛围的，说室内设计的艺术即是光线的艺术虽然有些夸大其词，但也不无道理。艺术的形式最终是通过视觉表达而传达于人的，尤其是强调视觉冲击力的展示设计。

这些设计的实现最终是依靠三维表现图向业主体现，同时设计师也是通过三维表现图来完善自己的设计。这样也就是表现图的优劣可以影响方案的成功，但并不是决定的因素，他只是辅助设计的一种手段、方法，千万不能本末倒置，过分地突出表现的效用，起决定作用的还应该是设计本身。

5.4.4 细部设计阶段

家具设施设计、装饰设计、灯具照明设计、门窗、墙面和顶棚连接展示内容的特殊表现都是依附于发展阶段的完善设计阶段。大部分的问题已经在发展阶段完成，这只是更加深入地与施工和预算结合。

施工图设计是设计的最后一项工作，纯技术的表现即可。

5.5 功能分区及展区布置

5.5.1 展示空间布局基本原则

（1）采用动态的、序列化的、有节奏的空间展示形式

展示空间最大的特点是具有很强的流动性，所以在空间设计上采

to is that the designer should use the dynamic, sequent and rhythmical exhibition form which is decided by the nature of the exhibition space and human factor. As visitors, human beings experience and have the ultimate spatial feelings while moving in the exhibition space. Therefore, the display space must take this fact as the base and arrange the visiting lines in the most reasonable way. As a matter of fact, the audience can participate in the exhibition activities in a mobile, integrate and economical way and do not repeat routes, particularly in important exhibition areas. In space disposal, designers should create a space layout as fluent as music, which is in measured tones with great fun and changes.

For example, the German exhibition room integrated enclosure with permeability, in Barcelona Exposition, Spain, which guided people to proceed along the visiting route formed by the partition layout after entering the exhibition space. When walking, people can see several levels of the space from different perspectives. Designers used dexterous space division methods so that the limited space became an infinite space, while the infinite space contained limitation. The constantly changing space orientation made the display smooth and rhythmic, so that people could enjoy the space of all dimensions in a constantly changing visual composition.

Chinese garden art is similar to the exhibition art from which we can gain some inspirations. For example, the garden is particular about the transfer in space sequence and the intermingling of the feeling and scene in the tour route. All of these are worthy of being used considering space exhibition forms.

用动态的、序列化的、有节奏的展示形式是首先要遵从的基本原则，这是由展示空间的性质和人的因素决定的。人在展示空间中处于参观运动的状态，是在运动中体验并获得最终的空间感受的，这就要求展示空间必须以此为依据，以最合理的方法安排观众的参观流线，使观众在流动中，完整地、经济地介入展示活动，尽可能不走或少走重复的路线，尤其是不在展示的重点区域内重复，在空间处理上做到犹如音乐旋律般的流畅，抑扬顿挫、分明有致.使整个设计顺理成章。在满足功能的同时，让人感受到空间变化的魅力和设计的无限趣味。

例如西班牙巴塞罗那博览会的德国馆是采用围中有透、透中有围，围透划分空间的处理手法，使人进入展览空间之后，沿隔断布置所形成的参观路线不断前进，在行进中，可以从不同的角度看到几个层次的空间。设计师在该馆的空间处理上，采用灵巧的划分空间的手法，使有限的空间变成无限，无限的空间中包含着有限，以不断变化着的空间导向，使整个空间的展示形式流畅、有节奏，让人们在不断变换的视觉构图中欣赏到全方位的空间。

中国的园林艺术在这点上与展示艺术有着异曲同工之妙，我们可以从中获得一些启发。如园林在空间序列上讲究启承转合，明暗开合；在游览路线上讲究移步换景，情景交融。这些都值得在考虑空间展示形式时采纳借鉴。

(2) Factor of Human Should be Considered so that Space Supplies Better Service to Human

The basic structure of exhibition space is composed of place structure, path structure and area structure, among which the place structure is the basic attribute because place reflects the basic relationship between human and space and it shows us the design is human-centered. The corporative "force" is formed by the center (or places), the direction (or path) and the area (or field). That is to say, human position is highlighted in the social and psychological state. It is human who has given the exhibition space the fourth dimension and practivity from abstract by moving in it. Meanwhile, people gain psychological feelings in the course of experiencing. "Human" is the ultimate object that exhibition space serves for, so the exhibition design must meet the spiritual demands of human beings as superior animals.

Display design have to meet people's material and spiritual needs, which is the fundamental basis for the analysis of exhibition space. Human needs a comfortable and harmonious display environment, good display effect with both sound and color, information-rich display content, safe and convenient space planning and thoughtful service facilities.etc. All these are human beings' spiritual demands for the exhibition design. Designers need to analyze the activities of visitors and give sufficient attention to ergonomics with scientific attitude in the design, so that the shape and size of the display space will be suitable for the human body and activities. This is the most basic space requirements. At the same time, since people need a

（2）在空间设计中考虑人的因素，使空间更好地服务于人

展示空间的基本结构由场所结构、路径结构、领域结构所组成，其中场所结构属性是展示空间的基本属性。因为场所反映了人与空间这个最基本的关系，它体现了以人为主体。通过中心（亦即场所）、方向（亦即路径）、区域（亦即领域）协同作用的关系"力"，即"突出了社会心理状态中人的位置"，是人赋予了展示空间的第四维性，使它从虚幻的状态通过人在展示环境中的行动显现出实在性，同时人在对这种空间的体验过程中，获得全部的心理感受。"人"是展示空间最终服务的对象，所以人作为高级动物在精神层面上的需求是展示设计必须满足的一个方面。

展示设计需要满足人在物质和精神上的双重需求，这是在进行展示空间分析时的基本依据。人类需要舒适和谐的展示环境，声色俱全的展示效果，信息丰富的展示内容，安全便捷的空间规划，考虑周到的服务设施等，这些都是人类在精神上对展示设计提出的要求。这就需要设计师仔细地分析参观者的活动行为并在设计中以科学的态度对人体工程学给予充分的重视，使展示空间的形状、尺寸与人体尺度之间有恰当的配合，使空间内各部分的比例尺度与人们在空间中行动和感知的方式配合得适宜、协调，这是最基本的空间要求。同时人们应该是在一个舒适的环境中进行活动，

comfortable environment, it will become a cold and mechanical body without life if the designer cannot provide people with a warm space even the space has used the most advanced display means. Only when the space display space full of humanity, it is a "sensible" and "reasonable" design.

(3) To Display Exhibits in the most Effective Space

Exhibits play the leading role in the exhibition space, and the primary purpose of space division is to display exhibits to the audience in the most effective places. Logical order and arrangement, rational allocation of exhibition areas should be adopted as the propriety of the exhibition. Therefore, designers must consider the space issue combining with the display contents, because different display contents have the corresponding display form and space division. For example, the commercial display requires more open space to improve interactive exchanges between spaces. The location of exhibits should be prominent and give people visual shock and strong impression by sound, light, electricity, dynamic simulation, and enough exhibition space etc. In short, to place exhibits in proper positions is the first consideration of space planning and also the key for a successful display design.

(4) To Guarantee the Safety of the Ancillary and Entire Space

Some largescate exhibitions may include such energy consumption equipment as various apparatuses, machinery, equipment and models The operation of such equipment needs some power, such as electricity, compressed air, steam and so on. These ancillary facilities also need to occupy certain space, so designers must

如果不能创造一个给人以心理上亲近温暖感觉的空间，即便是利用了最先进展示手段的环境，也只是冷冰冰的机械组成的没有生机的躯壳。一个充满人性化的展示空间才是一个"合情"、"合理"的设计。

（3）以最有效的空间位置展示展品

展品是展示空间的主角，以最有效的场所位置向观众呈现展品是划分空间的首要目的。逻辑地设计展示的秩序、编排展示的计划、对展区的合理分配是利用空间达到最佳展示效果的前提。因此，设计师必须将空间问题与展示的内容结合起来进行考虑，不同的展示内容有与之相对应的展示形式和空间划分。如商业性质的展示活动要求场地较为开阔，空间与空间之间相互渗透以便互动交流，展品的位置要显眼，对于那些展示视觉中心点如声、光、电、动态及模拟仿真等展示形式，要给以充分的、突出的展示空间，以增强对人的视觉冲击，给观众留下深刻的印象。总之，给展品以合理的位置是展示空间规划首要考虑的问题，也是能否做成一个成功的展示设计的关键。

（4）保证展示环境的辅助空间和整个空间的安全性

在一些大型的展示活动中，可能包括各种仪器、机械、装备及模型等需要消耗能源的设备。这些设备的运行大都需要一定的动力支持，如电力、压缩空气、蒸汽等，这些辅助设施也都需要占据一定的空间，而且必须考虑将这些设备的

consider isolating such space with display environment so as to prevent noise and harmful gas pollution.

In the process of space design, the needs of the audience are of primary importance. Therefore, we must attach importance to the safety of exhibition space. For instance, in the arrangement of visiting lines, designers must consider all the potential accidents such as power cut, fires, sudden disasters take some emergency measures. In large-scale exhibitions, there must be sufficient accesses, emergency evacuation directional signs and emergency lighting systems. In order to provide convenience for the audience, designers should also take into account the convenience for the audience's passage and rest, and the special needs of the handicapped to seek a "barrier-free" design which is also a trend of the development of modern exhibition design.

5.5.2 Function and Form of the Exhibition Space

(1) Division of the Main Functions

A. Public space is an area for public use and activities. There must be enough space for entry and exit so that it won't affect the other people's passage when some people stop to converse. Besides, there should be space for rest when necessary.

B. Information space: The area of information space is determined by number, size and flow of the exhibits. The exhibits should be placed scientifically, or visitors will feel more disappointed when they walk deeper to see more exhibits. The design of exhibition space should aim at attracting visitors.

C. Ancillary space:It refers to concealed or semi-concealed space which is not easy for visitors to notice, such as storage, workshop and reception room. A reception room, which is often located at the end of information space, is designed for the convenience of mutual exchanges and negotiations

空间与展示环境隔离开，以防止噪声、有害气体的污染，并做好安全防范。考虑好对这些辅助空间的处理是顺利完成整个展示活动的保障。

在空间设计的过程中，观众的需求是第一位的，所以必须重视展示空间的安全性。如参观流线的安排必须设想到各种可能发生的意外因素，如停电、火灾、意外灾害等，必须考虑到相应的应急措施。在大型的展示活动中，必须有足够的疏散通道和应急指示标识、应急照明系统等。为了给观众提供方便，展示的空间设计中要相应地考虑到观众的通行、休息的方便，尽可能地考虑到伤残者的特殊需求，以谋求"无障碍"设计，这也是现代展示设计发展的一个趋向。

5.5.2 展示空间的功能与形式

（1）展示空间主要功能区的划分

A. 公共空间：是供公众使用和活动的区域，要有足够的面积便于进出，在停留交谈时又不影响其他人出入，必要时还能提供休息的空间。

B. 信息空间：其大小由展品数量、大小和日流量决定。展品的陈列要有科学性，不要使参观者越往里看越失望。展示空间的设计要以吸引参观者为目的。

C. 辅助功能空间：是指参观者不容易觉察的地方，具隐秘性或半隐私性。如储藏间、工作间和接待间。其中接待间多为方便参展商与客户间相互交流洽谈而设计，常被安排在信息空间的结

between exhibitors and customers. It is set up as a prop in accordance with exhibition activities and has the same style as those activities.

(2) Types of the Overall Space

A. Outward Display Space: Known as "open (island) display space", the booth stands alone like an island and attracts the attention of visitors and can be entered from all directions. The structure of these booths is double-deck or three-deck making them magnificent and prominent.

B. Inward Display Space: Known as "closed-end display space", it is generally adopted by small booths. for it is easy to control the space form and cost. However, it is relatively difficult to decide content to attract visitors. A few larger display booths are designed to be closed-end display space. For example in the Seventh China International Fashion Exposition, the booth of the famous Chinese brand Baoxiniao was designed to be closed all around with only one entrance. Relying on its vast exhibition space and mode-making means of strong character, it also attracted many visitors and achieved good effect. No matter what space form it takes, a complete booth must be eye-catching and unusual.

(3) Methods of Handling Space Forms

A. Space Enclosure: In handling horizonal space, the designer should make a dear and reasonable distribution of all functional areas which should be harmonious both inside and outside with interesting forms. In the indoor exhibition space design, "space enclosures" is the most commonly used method which displays a variety of changes in commonness and simplicity through the latitude and longitude arrangements of props. When an exhibition is distributed in two different display spaces, the designer should use the method of space linkage in order to give

尾处，用与展示活动相统一的道具搭建，风格也相互和谐统一。

(2)总体空间形式的类型

A．外向式展示空间：亦称"敞开（岛屿）式展示空间"，展台就像小岛一样自成一体，它从各个方向吸引着参观者的注意力而且从四个方向都可以进入。这种展台的结构可以是双层的，也可以是三层的，气势宏大，个性突出。

B．内向式展示空间：亦称"封闭式展示空间"。一般小展台容易采用这种方法，由于展台面积小所以空间形式容易把握，造价相对低一些，但采用何种方式将参观者吸引入内却是比较难做的。也有个别面积大的展台做成封闭式的展示空间，像第七届中国国际服装服饰博览会中，报喜鸟展台的设计就是将四周围隔起来，只开了一个出入口，依靠其庞大的展示空间、极富个性的造型手段，同样也吸引了不少参观者，取得了不错的效果。所以无论采用哪一种空间形式，作为一个完整的展台必须是醒目而与众不同的。

（3）空间形式的处理手法

A．围隔、联系和渗透：水平横向空间处理中，应使各功能区的分配明确合理，内外通透和谐，形式丰富有趣。在室内展示空间设计中使用最普遍的手法即是"围隔空间法"。这种手法凭借对展示道具的经纬安排，在平凡朴素之中显现出千姿百态的变化。当一个展览内容分布在不同的场地，安排在不同的展示空间里时，为了给参观者一个总体印象，使参

visitors an overall impression so that they can associate the two spaces together. This method can make use of carpet extending, flowers placing, or similar color tone selection, which has both unity and the function of guidance. In modern exhibitions, many information space and negotiation space often use transparent or translucent glass walls to isolate from the outdoor space to form an integral whole. This method is called space infiltration, that is, "We are integrated with each other ".

B. Sharp Contrast:For an ordinary small booth, designers can employ the method of highlighting the height and brightness of the main space and lowering the ancillary space in order to attract the attention of visitors far away. Sharp contrast can easily achieve good effect and even influence the overall arrangement of space with proper use. Sometimes sharp contrast can be used to publish company image efficiently, with a erect extension, when the booth is not in a favorable position.

C. Structural Display: The formation of structural space is that structure displays the space form. The main forms of spatial structure interface include shells, tents, inflatable structure and grids, among which the most common form is grid. More space can be achieved by a triangle or foursquare cone, which is connected by the sphere nodes as a basic structural units. There is also a structural space composed of pyramidal structures which are welded out of steel and steel pipes. This structure is widely used for it can be dismantled and reused and is highlighted by era characteristics.

D. Curve Application: Organic space form is people's pursuit for the real form of the nature.

观者看完展览后能将两处的展览内容联系起来，就要使用联系空间法，可采用地毯一直延伸过去，或摆放彩带、盆花等，还可依靠相同色调的安排来显示，既有统一性又有导向功能。现代展览中，很多信息空间或会谈空间经常使用全透或半透玻璃幕墙与室外相隔，使展厅内外浑然一体,这种方法称为渗透空间法，即"你中有我，我中有你"。

B．强烈对比法：对于一般的小展台而言，在竖向空间处理中，为了吸引远处参观者的注意力可以采用突出主体的高大明亮而降低辅助空间的手法。将前面的一个展示空间降低形成强烈的对比形式，这种手法易出效果，使用得当，能左右全局的空间安排。有时由于场地位置不好，为了全面介绍宣传自己，可以采用沿垂直方向向上叠加层的手法扩大空间，目的在于更有效地宣传企业形象。

C．结构表现法：结构空间形成就是空间形式依靠结构来表现。结构空间的界面形态主要有壳体、篷帐、充气结构、网架等，其中以网架结构形式最为普遍。以基本结构单元为基础的球体节点，交接出三角锥体或四角锥体可创造出更大的空间；也有使用钢筋、钢管为材料焊接的锥体结构进行组合的结构空间。这种结构形式因其可拆卸和具重复使用性而得到广泛应用，这种形式还突出了时代特色且具有现代感。

D．曲线运用法：有机空间形式就是人们对自然界真实形态

Through the use of geometric and human body curves, people achieve the desire of returning to the nature. In today's booth designers, some designers use a large number of rough stones and logs, real mountain and water, waterfalls and flowers as decorating props, while others use a lot of free curves, surfaces and modern soft materials to give the limited space boundless creativity and changes.

(4) Scientific Execution

Before the execution of the design plan, designers should carefully consider the following questions: first, the issue of safety particularly fire safety issues. Generally, wood or cloth is prohibited from being directly exposed to the surface in the exhibition. If necessary, they must be sprayed with fireproof coatings. Secondly, the placement of exhibits should be scientific and logical to avoid disorder. Thirdly, the designer should consider in advance the potential wonderful scenes in the exhibition.

A. Space Design: This is the primary issue that designers will encounter. Designers should find out the spatial relationship between different exhibits or exhibitors and take this as an important base for space allocation and area distribution.

B. Plane Design: Plane design is the basis of exhibition design. All the new concepts related to the creation of artistic environment are highly synthesized through plane design to reflect a united and wonderful space. The plane design must give prominence to exhibits, distiriguish the subject and subordinate, unify and integrate all parts, have clear generatrix and concise lines. and be full of characteristics and novelty. Then beautiful plane form is naturally achieved after meeting all these requirements. In addition, designers should have a conscious pursuit, which may come from inspiration of natural forms or formal accumulation of people's accepted ideas through common practice

的追求。通过对几何曲线以及对人体曲线的运用完成回归自然的愿望，在当今的展台设计中，大量地使用了原石原木、真山真水、瀑布鲜花作装饰道具，有的还大量运用自由曲线、曲面以及现代软体材料，有限的空间中蕴含着无限的创造与变化。

（4）设计实施的科学性

在具体计划实施之前，应全面周密地考虑以下几个问题：第一是安全问题，特别是防火问题，展览中一般都禁止纯木或布料直接暴露在表面，如果需要暴露，也一定要喷上防火涂料；第二是展品的摆放要符合科学性与逻辑性，避免杂乱无章；第三是在设计时应预先想到展览会中可能出现的精彩场面。

A．空间规划：这是设计者遇到的首要问题，要搞清楚不同的展品或展出单位之间的空间关系，并以此作为空间配置与场地分配的重要依据。

B．平面设计：平面设计是展示设计的基础，一切有关展示艺术环境创造的创意思维都将通过平面设计实现高度的综合，展现统一而美妙的展示空间形象。平面设计必须达到突出展品、主从分明、整合统一、动线清晰简洁、通透合度、虚实相宜、富于特色、立意新颖。这些要求达到了，美的平面形式也就深含其中了。另外，设计时要有意识地追求某种形式感，这种形式感可能来自自然形态的启示，也可能来自人类约定俗成的抽象美感的形式积淀。对这些形式感

for abstract beauty. The pursuit of form sense should make the situation for best order and harmony from top to bottom, right to left, square and round, size and actual.

It is also essential to determine the sequence and visiting lines which have a scientific base. First of all, designers should arrange the trend of generatrix according to scientific procedure of internal development of exhibits. Secondly, designers must arrange lines according to the spatial relationships inherent in buildings and try to harmonize these two factors. At last, the routine can not be designed separately and should be handled together with the other items. The design of lines requires to be sequencial, brief, convenient and flexible.

C. Composition of Exhibition Space: Composition of exhibition space, also called creation of exhibition space, can be applied to the creation of exhibition building and particularly to specific exhibition space such as exhibition halls, areas, and booths. The elements, which restrict exhibition space, mainly are exhibition columns, top boards, exhibition panels, roofs, exhibition walls, show cases and glass platforms. Various space shapes are produced with each element or their combination. An exhibition space, which is in dynamic unity, will be developed in accordance with repetition and gradual change of these factors.

(5) Lighting, Lolor and Decorative Greening

A. Role of Lighting:Lighting plays an important role in exhibition, because all the beautiful shapes and colors rely on light to be transmited and the intensity of light directly influences overall effect of the booth. Light can be divided into two sources, natural light and artificial light. Because natural light is quite weak and tends to be influenced by natural factors, artificial lighting is applied to exhibitions to

的追求，要因势利导，做到上下、左右、方圆、大小、虚实处理等生动有序，和谐统一。

确定总的时序线路与参观线路也相当关键。这两条线路不是随心所欲的，而应是有科学依据的。首先要根据展品内容内在发展的科学程序安排动线的走向；其次要根据建筑物所固有的空间关系安排线路并尽量与之保持和谐；最后是要与其他各项一并处理，不要单独设计。线路的设计要求一是顺序性，二是简短便捷，三是灵活性。

C. 展示空间构成：展示空间构成就是展示空间的创造方法。这种方法可运用于展示建筑的创造中，而更多地运用于具体展示空间的创造过程中，如展厅、展示区、展示摊位。限定这些空间界面实体的形态要素主要有展柱、眉板、展板、顶棚、展墙、展柜、玻璃地台等，对这些要素进行无限制的分组编排则会产生各式各样空间形态，这些各式各样的构成形式按照重复渐变等构成手法予以拓展，就会出现一个统一而多变的展示空间形态。

（5）照明、色彩与装饰绿化

A.照明的重要作用：照明在展示中起着重要作用，一切美丽的形与色都依靠光线来传递，光线的强弱也直接影响着展台的整体效果。光线有自然光与人造光之分，但由于自然光较弱，又受自然因素的影响，现在展览都采用人工照明来烘托展览气氛。

foil exhibition atmosphere.

Requirements of exhibition lighting are as follows: First, to provide a comfortable visual environment in which the exhibits have sufficient brightness, clarity and a reasonable perspective of view; Second, to ensure the security of power supply system, reducing damage of light to exhibits and injury to visitors; Third, to give distinct characteristics of the age we live in. The main feature of basal lighting is that it is evenly-distributed making public space appear relatively unified and harmonious. Local lighting is intended to highlight the exhibits so as to attract the attention of visitors and leave deep impression on them. It is suitable to be applied to unfixed situations such as non-border display area or variable sized exhibits. It is flexible and adaptable, and plays an important role in highlighting key points. The purpose of decorative lighting is to foil atmosphere of the display area, enrich color sense of space and layers, and create different lighting effects with color filter so that visitors will feel curious and are attracted to have a view.

B. Role of Color: Where there is light, there is color; where there is color, there is shape When there is shape, people can fully sense the wonderfulnes of space. There are numerous colors in the nature, for about 7500000 to 10000000 kinds, but only tens or hundreds of kinds are commonly used by people. Colors can not only express people's feelings, but also affect people's emotions. As a matter of fact, colors can be distributed depending on different feeling requirements. Red stimulates people, promote them to chat and enhance their appetites; orange makes people happy; yellow has the highest brightness and is as warm as the sun; green, which is cool, fresh and elegant, represents nature and gives youth a sense of security and life; blue stands for calmness and wisdom, and makes people think of clean water and blue sky and coolness.

展示照明的要求有：第一，提供舒适的视觉环境，使展品有足够的亮度、观赏清晰度和合理的观赏角度；第二，确保供电系统的安全性，减少光线对展品的损坏和对参观者的损伤；第三，使照明方式和光照具有鲜明的时代特色。基础照明的特点是光线分布比较均匀，使公共空间显得比较统一与和谐；局部照明的目的在于突出展品，令其吸引参观者的注意力，并加深印象，适用于展示场地及展品尺寸不固定的情况，灵活性大、适应性强，并且对突出重点能起到很好的作用。装饰照明的目的是烘托展示场地的气氛，丰富空间的色彩感和层次感，还可以装滤色片制造出不同的灯光效果，以使参观者产生好奇心并吸引其驻足参观。

B. 色彩的作用：色彩是光的反射，有光才能看到色，有色才能看到形，有形才能充分感觉空间的美妙。自然界色彩繁多，有750万到1000万种，人们经常使用的不过几十种到上百种。色彩不仅能表达感情，还能影响人们的情绪，在运用的过程中，可依靠不同的色彩带给人的不同感受而进行分布使用。如红色使人振奋，能促进交谈，增进食欲；橙色使人快乐；黄色明度最高，有如阳光般温暖；绿色冷静、清新、雅致，给人安全感和青春生命之感，代表大自然；蓝色冷静、智慧，使人想到水和蓝天的清洁和凉意等。

Designers should pay attention to the uniformity of color distribution. Each booth must have a dominant color tone. Under the premise of uniformity, the use of color in various functional areas should be differentiated, but this distinction should be coordinated and orderly. The use of color in local areas plays an ancillary and secondary role, which should be prevented from superseding the primary. Designers should be bold in using colors for no color is superior or inferior. According to color allocation theory, the designers should try to achieve the effect of "Elegance generates beauty"by means of free selection and harmonious application. Especially for the use of non-color series, black, white and grey it is a trend in the future because of the rapid rhythm of modern life, too much information and fast changes in the objective environment.Since people desire to pursue tranquility and serenity in their hearts, all the visible tinted objects will be lively and full of vitality. in the environment of black, white and grey.

C. Role of Decoration and Greening:The display environment cannot survive without decoration and greening which are the organic components of the overall creative process of space exhibition. Decoration is used to stress space patterns and exhibition function. Greening is not only a kind of decoration, but reflects ecological significance. Decoration should be limited so as to improve the display system and function.

5.6 Display Effect Picture

The design displays the contents to the audience purposefully and logically through using space planning, layout, lighting control, color scheme and the planning of various organizations in the design, and tries to make the audience accept the information conveyed in the design.

对色彩的计划分布，要注意统一性，每个展台都要有一个主色调，在统一色调的前提下，各功能区的用色要有所区别，但这种区别应是协调的、有规律的。局部色彩的运用，是起辅助作用的，严禁"喧宾夺主"。使用色彩要大胆，色彩本身无优劣之分，要依靠色彩的配置原理，自由选择，和谐运用，争取达到"以雅为美"的韵致。特别是对无色彩系列——黑、白、灰色的运用，是未来发展的趋势，因为当代生活节奏过速，各种信息太多，客观环境变化太快，人们在内心深处滋生了对淡然静谧的追求，在黑白灰的环境里，一切有形有色的物体都会显得生动而富于活力。

C. 装饰绿化的作用：在展示环境中不能没有装饰与绿化，它们是展示空间整体创造过程的有机组成部分。装饰只为强调空间形态和展示功能，绿化既是装饰又体现生态意义。装饰不能漫无限制地使用，要有所节制，以达到完善展示系统和突出展示功能的目的。

5.6 展示设计的效果图

通过设计，运用空间规划、平面布置、灯光控制、色彩配置以及各种组织策划，有计划、有目的、符合逻辑地将展示的内容展现给观众，并力求使观众接受设计所计划传达的信息。

5.6.1 Technique of Effect Drawing

The exhibition effect picture refers to the modeling method of three-dimensional space to make a creative expression of exhibition design as an exchange media.

5.6.2 Classification of Effect Drawing

(1) Overall Effect Drawing

This refers to a drawing that can demonstrate the whole exhibition area or the environment, space, color, props, and exhibits. It is also an expression of the relationship of scale, region, shape, color and other information.

(2) Local Effect Drawing

This refers to the drawing demonstrating local effect of the exhibition hall.

(3) Axonometric Effect Drawing

This is also called axonometric drawing. It is not a perspective drawing, but a parallel projection drawing.

(4) Perspective Effect Drawing

As a perspective drawing pays great attention to the perspective effects of space modeling, designers should not only master the drawing techniques of vision habits and perspective laws, but also be familiar with the tools, materials, techniques and procedures of how to draw the effect picture. Here are some methods: one point, two points and three points' perspective drawing.

Apart from considering the display of goods, designers must ensure a certain degree of negotiation and sales space in the space design.

5.6.1 效果图的概念

展示效果图是指利用立体空间的造型方法，进行展示设计的创意表达，同时作为一种交流媒介。

5.6.2 效果图的分类

（1）整体效果图

是指在一张图纸上，能够把整个展区或展馆的环境、空间、色彩、道具、展品陈列及其具有的规模、区域关系、形态关系、色彩关系等信息表达出来。

（2）局部效果图

指展示场馆的局部效果的图纸。

（3）轴侧效果图

又称为轴侧图，不是透视图，而是平行投影图。

（4）透视效果图

透视效果图注重的是空间造型的透视效果，所以设计人员不仅要掌握符合视觉习惯和透视规律的画法，同时也要熟悉和掌握绘制效果图的工具、材料、技法和程序。其方法有：一点透视画法、二点透视画法、三点透视画法。

在设计上除了考虑商品的展示外，还必须考虑在空间的设计上保证具有一定的洽谈和销售空间。

Chapter 6
Landscape Elements Design

第6章
景观小品设计

6.1 Concept

Generally speaking, landscape elements usually refer to all the artificial structures of indoor and outdoor environment with a sense of beauty, which are set up for the needs of environment. It is also called garden furniture, urban furniture, street furniture and urban elementsetc.

In recent years, with the hosting of the Olympic Games and Shanghai World Exposition, the role of landscape elements in garden has been well-known. More and more landscape elements have appeared in modern urban landscape construction, which have strong decorative effect and relatively small size. With the development of modern scientific techniques and art, requirement for landscape elements becomes higher and higher. In the rapid development of urban construction, landscape elements are reflecting the city's taste and high spiritual civilization with overflowing details. Landscape elements are developing in a more artistic, scientific and technological direction with more prominent characteristics, combining more harmoniously with the environment.

6.2 Characteristics of Landscape Elements

6.2.1 Harmony and Unity

Landscape elements are always in a certain environment which might be indoor or outdoor environment. Landscape element should match and integrate with the surrounding environment

6.1 概念

景观小品，一般泛指建筑室内、室外环境中一切具有一定美感的，为环境所需而设置的人为构筑物。也有人称之为园地装置、城市装置、街道家具、城市元素等。

随着近年来奥运会的举办和上海世博会的隆重造势，景观小品在园林景观中的作用已越来越为众人所熟知，装饰性强而且体积相对较小的景观小品正越来越密切地溶入现代城市的景观建设中。随着现代化科技手段不断创新，人们对景观小品功能要求越来越高，景观小品正在向着艺术性更强、科技性更高、特征性更强、与环境的结合能力更和谐的方向发展，在城市建设的飞速发展中，正以充满魅力的细节展现着城市的品位与精神文明。

6.2 景观小品的特征

6.2.1 和谐统一性

一个景观小品作品总是依附于一个特定的环境，可能是室内也可能是室外，这就要求景观小品要与周围环境相匹配相融合，

to create a harmonious atmosphere as a whole. Therefore, the designer should investigate the surrounding environment, architectural style and regional function before carrying out the design. Landscape elements are in harmony and unity with the surrounding environment while adding lustre to it, in details. Conflicts or contradictions between environmental elements and their surrounding environment should be avoided in form, style, color and texture design etc. We need to remember the whole environment is the hero in the whole design, while environmental element should not only add something to local environment, but bring aesthetics to the environment as an element.

6.2.2 Reflection of Artistic Beauty

Artistic beauty is an important nature of elements in large environment. The beautiful expressions of elements are mainly reflected by material quality, texture and color.

Landscape elements design and operation require attention of expression of the elements' rhythm and shape, then certain aesthetic depth can be achieved by shape fluency, color, choice and contrast of materials, size and scale etc.

6.2.3 Expression of Local Culture

Different regional culture are consisted of various factors,such as climate, general configuration of the earth's surface, architecture, social customs, ways of life, thinking habits, folk traditions, religion and culture. Because people of different times and areas have different understanding of aesthetics and culture, the elements design reflects the social, regional and folk aesthetic taste of their area.Therefore, the design process of elements is the process of refining of regional and cultural connotations,

从而形成一个整体和谐的环境氛围。因此，在小品创作之初就要考察其周边环境、附近区域的功能和建筑风格，保证环境小品设计元素要与周边环境相和谐、统一，从细节上为环境增光添彩；避免小品在形式、风格、色彩、材质等方面的设计上与周边环境的要素产生冲突或对立。设立景观小品的目的在于实现整个环境景观的艺术美感，而不是仅仅在环境的局部增添某样东西。时刻谨记整体环境是这场设计中的主角，而单体小品则是为了环境的整体和谐利益而从属于环境景观的一个元素。

6.2.2 艺术美感的体现

处在大环境中的小品，艺术美感是其重要属性。它的美感主要通过以下几个方面得以体现：小品本身的造型、材质、肌理、色彩等方面。

景观小品的设计与制作，须注意其形态韵律的体现，使其在造型流畅度、色彩的运用、材质的选择对比、规模尺度等方面都有一定的审美深度。

6.2.3 地域文化的表达

气候地貌、建筑风格、社会习俗、生活方式、思维习惯、民俗传统、宗教文化等诸多因素构成了不同的地域文化，而且不同时期人们对于美学文化的理解各有差异，所以小品的设计受到了上述因素的影响，同时也反映了其所在地域的社会、地域、民俗的审美情趣。因此，小品的设计过程就是地域文化内涵精炼提纯

环境艺术设计专业英语教程

for regional characteristic of environmental elements often reflects in the aspect of external image. It is well-known that buildings take on various architectural styles because of the different cultural background and geographical characteristics. The design of environmental elements should be like this in order to achieve a cultural integration with local humanities and customs. As the embodiment of style also has a theme, we should refine a theme to express and extend it to be an organic entity with formal beauty and regional culture. Otherwise, it is difficult for simple form of representation and symbols. to arouse the sympathy of people's soul.

6.2.4 Reflection of Functional Variety

Various landscape elements not only reflects beauty in form, local culture and scientific design, but also have functions of enriching environment and creating a space atmosphere. For example, some stone or bronze sculptures can be set near the seats for rest, in special shapes such as chessboard, pets and person images, or some other elements with lively theme, which can attract tourists to participate in or take photographs. It can be interactive. flexible, diverse, vivid and smart.

6.3 Category and Collocation of Elements

6.3.1 Concept and Features of Garden Architecture Elements

Garden elements are small architecture facilities to provide service, facilitate greening management and have decoration, display, lighting and rest functions. They are characterized by small size, rich forms and various functions.

(1) Types of Garden Elements

A. Service Elements: Service elements are pavilions, gallery shelves, chairs, telephone

的过程，地域风情特征往往反映在环境小品外在形象上。众所周知，建筑物可以因为周围的文化背景和地域特征的不同而呈现出多样的建筑风格；环境小品的设计亦应如此，与本地区的人文风情达到一个文化融合的层次。风格的体现也是有主题的，我们应该把要表达的思想内涵提炼出一个主题，使这个主题延伸成一个具有形式美感和地域文化的有机实体，否则，单纯地做一些表象的形式与符号是很难激起人们心灵上的共鸣的。

6.2.4 功能的多样化

景观小品的多样性不仅体现在形式的美感、地域文化、科学设计上，还可以通过多样化的创意在某些特定的地点和场合起到丰富环境、营造空间氛围等功能。例如，在一些休息座椅附近做一些石质或铜质的雕塑作品，像棋盘、宠物、生活中的人物形象等，灵活多样、造型活泼，也可以吸引游客参与或拍照，增强景观与游人互动性。

6.3 小品类别及搭配

6.3.1 园林建筑小品

园林建筑小品是在园林绿地中为市民提供服务功能，方便绿化管理，用作装饰、展示、照明、休息等的小型建筑设施。它的特征是体量较小、造型丰富、功能多样、富有特色。

（1）园林建筑小品分类

A．服务小品：供游人休息、遮阳用的亭、廊架、座椅，为游

booths, hand-washing pools and dustbins, which can provide people with places to have a rest or other conveniences.

B. Decoration Elements: Decoration elements refer to sculptures, pavements, landscape walls, windows, doors and railings in various types of green space, some of which also have some other functions.

C. Display Elements: Display elements refer to various bulletin boards, tour guide maps, guidance signs and sign boards etc., which have function of propaganda, direction and education.

D. Illumination Elements: Illumination elements refer to lawn lights, square lights, landscape lights, courtyard lights and steamer lights.

(2) Garden Elements Design

Garden landscape has to meet technical and aesthetical requirements of garden architecture at the same time. When designing, the designer should coordinate aesthetics shape and space to create harmony. Therefore, we should pay attention to the following points:

A. Ingenious Orientation: As part of local landscape, garden elements should not only be elegant in its own form, but also have a profound meaning to express certain taste. This requires designers to conceive cleverly to integrate the environment, context and conception into a whole design.

B. Suitability: As a decoration of garden landscape, garden elements should occupy a small area. Generally, they should be designed to match the environment in size and dimention. For instance, huge lamps has to be installed in a large square to emit bright light, illuminating from high above; while small delicate lights are proper to be installed on both sides of a small avenue.

人服务的电话亭、洗手池等，为保持环境卫生的废物箱等。

B．装饰小品：各类绿地中的雕塑、铺装、景墙、窗、门、栏杆等，有的也兼具其他功能。

C．展示小品：各种布告栏、导游图、指路标牌、说明牌等，起到一定的宣传、指示、教育的功能。

D．照明小品：以草坪灯、广场灯、景观灯、庭院灯、射灯等为主的灯饰小品。

（2）园林建筑小品创意规则

园林景观中，除了园林建筑小品以外的局部城市细节设计，它既要符合园林建筑技术的要求，又要满足造型艺术和空间组合上的美感要求。设计时应把握好个体的艺术造型性和其在空间组合上的协调性。在设计上，我们应注意以下几点：

A．巧于立意：园林小品作为园林景物的一部分，在小环境中是一个主体，不仅要有形式美，还要具有深刻的内涵，表达一定的意境和情趣。这就要求设计者巧于构思，力求将物境、情境、意境融为一体。

B．精在体宜：园林小品作为园林景观的陪衬，在景观中所占面积不宜过大。一般在体量上力求与环境相适宜，根据环境空间选择相应的体量与尺度进行设计。如在大广场中，设巨型灯具，有明灯高照的效果，而在小的林阴曲径旁，只宜设小型园灯，不但要求体量小，

Another example, sizes of fountains and flower beds should be based on size of its corresponding space .

C. Highlighting Characteristics: Decorative elements of garden buildings should highlight local features, landscape features and artistic characteristics of monoscapes, providing themselves with unique styles. It should avoid dully repetition by all means. For example, a traditional Chinese pot-shaped fountain on a lawn can have a colorful view, when integrating with grasses and flowers into a unique whole.

D. Artistic Quality: The artistic quality of garden elements refers to aesthetic chateristics, which is a higher pursuit. Garden elements should meet the basic requirements of aesthetics, which display in two-dimensional or three-dimensional spatial artistic shapes. Garden elements should also take color, material and texture into consideration.

E. Technicality: Technology is the guarantee of the design, which requires the design to take full account of its implementation at the same time. The technical aspect requires considering elements' economy and applicability, actions of further management, cleaness and maintenance. It also need to respect the natural development process and promote recycling of resources to realize self-maintenance.

(3) Garden Plants and Allocation Methods of Building Elements

A. Plant Allocation Highlights the Theme of Building Elements: In green space of gardens, many building elements are functional entities with special cultural and spiritual connotations. For example, decorative elements such as sculptures, landscape walls and pavements have a special role and importance in different environment contexts. In classical gardens, allocations of leaking windows, moon gates and plants complement each other, enriching the artistic conception of the garden.

造型更应精致。喷泉、花池的体量等，都应根据所处的地域大小确定其相应的体量。

C. 突出特色：园林建筑装饰小品应突出地方特色、园林特色及单体的艺术特色，使其有独特的格调，切忌生搬硬套，产生雷同。如某园草地一侧，设置一中国传统的泡壶形喷泉，造型手法色彩鲜明，与花卉绿草融成一体，独具特色。

D. 注重艺术性：园林小品的艺术性是指其所呈现的美学特征，是较高层次的追求。园林小品不仅要注重主题和创意的表达方式，还要充分考虑色彩、材料、质感等方面的内容。

E. 注重技术性：技术是设计的保障，同时又要求设计应充分考虑其可实施性。技术层面既要考虑小品的经济性和可行性，后期管理、清洁和维护，还要做到尊重自然发展过程，倡导能源和物质的循环利用及自我维护。

（3）园林植物与建筑小品配置方法

A. 植物配置突出建筑小品主题：在园林绿地中，许多建筑小品都是具备特定文化和精神内涵的功能实体，如装饰性小品中的雕塑物、景墙、铺地，在不同的环境背景下表达了特殊的作用和意义。在古典园林中，漏窗、月洞门和植物相得益彰地配置，其包含的意境就更加丰富了。园林植物配置，也要通过选择合适的物

The plant design should highlight the main idea and spiritual connotation of the elements through choosing right plant species and allocation methods. For example, pavement with ice cracks pattern symbolizes the arrival of winter, so surrounding areas should be decorated by plants of winter echo. Accordingly, surrounding area can be covered by winter flowerer plants, such as Chimonanthus praecox's, Chinese plum flowers, bandanas with red fruits, and evergreen plants such as conifers and bamboo, so that the elements echo can integrate with each other and partment to reflect theme of the landscape. Another example, sculptures in memory of revolutionary martyrs should take color-leaved trees as background, because golden and red colors in autumn will thoroughly foil solemn commemoration atmosphere. If arrangement of architecture elements and plants is properly handled, it can not only create beautiful harmonious landscape, but also highlight the effect that cannot be achieved by any one of them.

B. Plant Allocation Coordinates Architecture Elements and Surrounding Environment: When architecture elements are not in harmony with surrounding green space in modeling, scale and colors etc., plants can be used to ease or eliminate such conflicts. For instance, lights for illumination is an essential facility in garden, but they will influence visual effect of greenspace regardless of its distribution and amount. Therefore, we can combine plant allocation with lighting to solve this problem. Lawn lights, square lights, landscape lights, courtyard lights and steamer lights can be installed in low shrubs, under tall trees or on the edge of plant communities without affecting light illumination at night. In addition, plants can also solve the same problems caused by some

种和配置方式来突出、衬托或者烘托小品本身的主旨和精神内涵。例如，冰裂纹铺地象征冬天的到来，在铺装周围的绿地区域中选择冬季季相特征的植物能够呼应小品的象征意义，如冬季开花的腊梅、梅花、挂红果的南天竹、常青的松柏类、竹类植物，与冰裂纹铺地一起可以起到彼此呼应、相互融合体现景观所要表现的主题。又如纪念革命烈士为主题的雕塑物以色叶树丛作为背景，一到秋天，色叶树的金色和红色把庄严凝重的纪念氛围渲染得淋漓尽致。建筑小品与植物一起配置，处理得当，不仅可以获得和谐优美的景观，而且还可突出单体所达不到的功能效果。

B. 植物配置协调建筑小品与周边环境的关系：建筑小品因造型、尺度、色彩等原因与周围环境不相称时，可以用植物来缓和或者消除这种矛盾。如以照明功能为主的灯饰，在园林中是一项不可或缺的基础设施，但是由于它分布较广、数量较多，在选择位置上如果不考虑与其他园林要素结合，那将会影响整体景观效果，利用植物配置和灯饰的结合设计可以解决这个矛盾。将草坪灯、景观灯、庭院灯、射灯等设计在低矮的灌木植物丛中、高大的乔木下或者植物群落的边缘位置，既起到了隐蔽作用又不影响灯光的夜间照明。另外，园林中还有些功能性的设施小品如垃圾桶、厕所等，假如设置的位置不合

functional facilities, such as trash cans and toilets etc. in improper places.

Furthermore, plant allocation can not only solve problems, but harmonize and beautify architecture elements and environment in garden. For instance, a kiosk taking dense woods as background is better than the one alone on lawn or hard ground, because it seems more natural and gives people more sense of safety. In Songjiang Square Tower Garden, Shanghai, it adds more wild taste of urban forest that a thatched pavilion built without any artificial marks against a bamboo forest.

C. Plant Allocation Enriches Artistic Composition of Building Elements: Generally speaking, contour lines of architecture elements, particularly kiosk, rectangular stools and landscape walls of large size, are relatively stiff and straight. However, with their beautiful gestures, soft foliage, rich natural colors and various seasonal aspects, plants can soften the borders, enrich artistic composition and add natural beauty of building elements, so as to make the overall environment appear harmonious and orderly regardless of dynamic or static enviroment.

Plant allocation is most effective to soften corners of architecture elements. It is better to choose shrubs and ground cover for people to appreciate flowers, foliage or fruit. We can also make a terrain to form a relatively stable and lasting landscape by adding one or several lush trees. Landscape walls, railings and curbstones mainly play roles of separation and decoration. Vines and low ground cover plants are often planted from their nature, which can not only soften, cover and obstruct the lines, but beautify the environment and provide fun for visitors to get close to the nature.

适也会影响到景观，也可以借助植物配置来处理和改变这些问题。

此外，植物配置不仅可以解决客观存在的问题，而且也可以配合建筑小品使园林中的景观和环境显得更为和谐、优美。如休息亭以浓郁、成片的树林为背景或以常绿树丛隐于其中，比单独放在一片草坪或者硬地上，在景观上要显得更加自然、不突兀，对于游人来说这样的休息亭也更易靠近、更具有安全感。在上海松江方塔园中，利用不加任何人工斧凿而建的茅草亭在一片竹林掩映之下，更加具有都市森林之野趣。

C. 植物配置丰富建筑小品的艺术构图：一般来说，建筑小品特别是体量较大的休息亭、长方形的坐凳、景墙等的轮廓线都比较生硬、平直，而植物以其优美的姿态、柔和的枝叶、丰富的自然颜色、多变的季相景观可以软化建筑小品的边界，丰富艺术构图，增添建筑小品的自然美，从而使整体环境显得和谐有序、动静皆宜。

特别是建筑小品的角隅，通过植物配置进行缓和柔化最为有效，宜选择观花、观叶、观果类的灌木和地被、草本植物成丛种植，也可略作地形，高处增添一至几株浓荫乔木组成相对稳定持久的景观。景墙、栏杆、道牙主要起到分隔和装饰的作用，在进行植物配置时常种植爬藤类、低矮地被植物使其自然攀援，这样不仅柔化、覆盖、遮挡了建筑小品硬质的棱角线条，而且也美化了环境，为游人增添了亲近自然之趣。

Light colors of grey series are more common used in architecture elements, which might be plodding. The color of architecture element could be complemented by green, color-leaf plants or plants of various patterns or seasonal changes, which adds linguistic expression for the function and connotation of building elements.

D. Plant Improves Function of Building Elements: Good plant allocation can not only beautify building elements, but also improve their functions. For example, several special trees next to directive elements (tour maps, guiding signs) can play the role of tour guides; vines planted in gallery greatly improve the shelter effect and function. Seats are elements widely distributed in garden. Their main function is for visitors to rest while viewing the scenery. Plant allocation near seats should be able to provide shelter in summer and no shadow in winter. Therefore, tall and deciduous trees can bring shade to seat and their big and tall crowns are "lens hoods" for visitors viewing scenery, which makes perspective vision clearer, more distinct and opener.

6.3.2 Pavement Elements

(1) Classification of Pavements

Ground occupies a large part of space, which is worthy of paying attention to when designing landscape. Ground pavement elements mainly rely on different textures and patterns of combinations of various materials to decorate the overall environment. The following are some common pavements:

A. Integral Pavement: Integral pavement refers to cement concrete or bituminous concrete pavement. It is plane, pressure-proof and wears proof, which is used for passage of vehicles and large people flow.

B. Block Materials: This type includes

另外，建筑小品一般为淡色、灰色系列居多，而绿色的、色叶类的、带有各种花色和季相变化的植物和建筑小品的结合，可以弥补它们单调的色彩，为建筑小品的功能和内涵表现增添另一种语言的表达。

D. 植物配置完善建筑小品的功能：好的植物配置不仅起到美化建筑小品的作用，而且还可以通过配置更加完善建筑小品本身的功能。如指示小品（导游图、指路标牌）旁的几棵特别的树可以起到指示导游的作用；在廊架上栽植攀援类植物，更加完善了廊架蔽荫的效果和功能。座椅是园林中分布最广、数量最多的小品，其主要功能是为游人休息、赏景提供停歇处。从功能完善的角度来设计，座椅边的植物配置应该要做到夏可蔽荫、冬不蔽日。所以座椅设在落叶大乔木下不仅可以带来阴凉，植物高大的树冠也可以作为赏景的"遮光罩"，使透视远景更加明快清晰，使休息者感到空间更加开阔。

6.3.2 地铺小品

（1）地面铺装分类

在空间组成中，地面比例很大，因此地面的装饰在景观设计中是值得重视的一个重要部分。地面铺装小品主要依靠各种材质组合成不同的纹理图案来装饰整体环境。常见的有：

A. 整体路面：指用水泥混凝土或沥青混凝土进行统铺的地面，平整、耐压、耐磨，用于通行车辆或人流集中的路线。

B. 块料铺地：包括各种天然

pavements made of all kinds of natural blocks or precast concrete blocks. It is solid, stable, and easy to walk on with colorful patterns, which is suitable for sidewalks in park or passage for light vehicles.

C. Broken Materials: This type refers to pavements made of all kinds of rubbles, tiles and pebbles etc. to form beautiful ground patterns. Being economic, beautiful and decorative, it is mainly used in sideways of all kinds of gardens and recreation places.

(2) Main Points for Pavement Design

Since characteristics of space usage, vehicles and people are different, we should note the following main points in ground pavement design:

A. Appropriate Pavement Materials: Appropriate materials should be in accordance with the nature, size, and characteristics of environmental space and construction cost of the project.

B. Exterior Design: Exterior design should be paid attention to, including scale, color and texture, and avoid conflict with the other environmental factors.

C. Combination with Soft Pavement: Ground landscape will become vivid and richful by combining hard pavement with lawn and greening.

6.3.3 Waterscape Elements

There are famous poems and idioms about Chinese gardens:"Water is the blood of earth, which flows in the arteries and veins" and "No water, no landscape". These sentences showed us how important water is to decorate landscape. Waterscape plays a special role in the environmental landscape and can always be an attractive view for people. The forms of waterscape include natural waterscape, garden-style waterscape, swimming-pool style waterscape and decorative waterscape, which vary in shapes and forms.

块料或各种预制混凝土块料铺地，坚固、平稳、便于行走，图案的纹样和色彩丰富多彩，适用于公园步行路，或少量轻型车路段。

C. 碎料铺地：用各种碎石、瓦片、鹅卵石等拼砌形成美丽的地纹，主要用于庭院和各种游憩、散步的小路，经济、美丽而富有装饰性。

（2）地面铺装设计要点

因为空间的使用性质不同，过往通行的车辆或人群也不相同，因此，在进行地面的铺装设计时，应注意以下几点：

A. 选择合适的铺地材料：根据环境空间的性质、规模、特点以及工程造价来确定适合的材料。

B. 注重铺地材料的外观设计：注意外观效果、尺度、色彩、质感；避免与环境中的其他要素冲突。

C. 注意与软式铺地结合：硬质铺地与草坪、绿化有机结合，相互穿插，以使地面景观生动丰富。

6.3.3 水景小品

中国园林素有"水者，地之学气，如筋脉之流动"，"无水不成景"之说，水对于景观的重要性由此可见一斑。水景在环境景观中起到了非同一般的作用，在众多小品中总是成为吸引人的一个亮点，人们总是喜欢围绕在水景周边欣赏、玩耍和嬉戏。水景的形式主要有自然式水景、园林式水景、泳池式水景、装饰式水景等形式，其中的具体造型又各有变化。

(1) Natural Waterscape

Constituents of Natural Waterscape:

Landscape constituent	Contents
Water body	Flow direction, color, inverted image, streams and water sources
Revetment	Roads along waters, buildings along banks(docks, ancient architecture), beaches and stone sculptures
Structure across waters	Bridges, trestles and ropeways
Aquatic plants (distant view)	Mountains, hills, cliffs and woods
Aquatic plants and animals	Phytoplankton, underwater plants, fish and birds
Sky and light	Refraction and diffusion, sprays and clouds

A. Revetment: Revetment is an importment part in hydrophilic landscape. Revetment landscape design should be based on specific situations, conditions and volume of waters(Fig. 6-1~Fig.6-6) . Revetment of large landscape or garden should be simple and open with water, roads and gentle grass slopes and trees. Pond haugh can be delicate with colorful grass and flowers and stones. It is also an important aspect to select material according to revement types .

Whether revetment and water lines are harmonious with the environment, it not only depends on types of revetment and materials, but also on the height between revetment and the water surface. Revetment should be designed as close as possible to water surface to meet people's hydrophilic demands, regardless of size and form. Other hydrophilic facilities (water platform, haugh, trestles and cable ropes) in the scenic spots should also be designed on the basis of scale relationship between human and waters.

B. Landscape Bridges: Landscape bridges consist Steel Bridge (Fig.6-7), Concrete Bridge (Fig.6-8), Arch Bridge (Fig.6-9), Log Bridge (Fig.6-10), Imitation Wood Bridge (Fig.6-11), Lumber Wood Bridge (Fig.6-12), Suspension Bridge (Fig.6-13), etc.

（1）自然式水景

自然水景的构成元素（详见下表）：

景观元素	内容
水体	水体流向、水体色彩、水体倒影、溪流、水源
驳岸	沿水道路、沿岸建筑（码头、古建等）、沙滩、雕石
水上跨越结构	桥梁、栈桥、索道
水生山体树木(远景)	山岳、丘陵、峭壁、林木
水生动植物（近景）	水面浮生植物、水下植物、鱼鸟类
天光映衬	光线折射漫射、水雾、云彩

A．驳岸：驳岸是亲水景观中应重点处理的部位，驳岸的景观应根据园区水体、水态及水量的具体情况而定（图6-1～图6-6）。大型的风景区或园林的水面，驳岸景观一般比较简洁、开阔，水、路、草坡与树林可以组成十分醒目而美丽的水景；水池驳岸要求布置细致，与各色花草、石块相结合。驳岸的类型与材料相互搭配也是驳岸设计的一项重要内容。

驳岸与水线形成的连续景观是否能与环境相协调，不但取决于驳岸的大小、类型及材料，还取决驳岸与水面的高度。对于旅游景区的沿水驳岸设计，不论规模大小及形式的不同，驳岸的高度及设计都应满足人的亲水性要求，尽可能贴近水面，游区中的其他亲水设施（水上平台、汀步、栈桥、栏索等）也应以人与水体的尺度关系为基准进行设计。

B．景观桥：景观桥一般分为钢制桥（图6-7）、混凝土桥（图6-8）、拱桥（图6-9）、原木桥（图6-10）、仿木桥（6-11）、锯材木桥（图6-12）、吊桥（图6-13）等。

环境艺术设计专业英语教程

Bridges play an indispensable role in natural and artificial waterscape. Bridges have multiple functions, such as forming a traffic crossing and regional signs; dividing rivers and water space; and becoming a place of river view. An unique shape can also give the bridge its own artistic value.

C. Plank Road: The Plank Road Above Water provides a multi-functional place for people to have a walk, rest, view landscape and exchange their minds. (Fig.6-14, Fig.6-15) Since the wood material has a flexible and simple texture, it is more comfortable than other materials. The surface of plank road is usually made up of panels (or intensively arranged wooden battens) and wooden frames. Eucalyptus wood, teak, fir and pine wood etc. are often used for plank road.

Waterscape design of the garden in the scenic spot should use various forms of the water to create an atmosphere of the scenic areas. Its characteristics are as follows:

桥在自然水景和人工水景中都起到不可缺少的景观作用，例如形成交通跨越，分割河流和水面空间，作为地区标志物、眺望河流和水面的良好场所，使其独特的造型具有自身的艺术价值。

C. 木栈道：临水木栈道为人们提供了行走、休息、欣赏景观和交流的多功能场所（图6-14、图6-15）。由于木板材料本身具有一定的弹性和朴实的质感，因此在上面行走较其他材料更为舒适。其表面由平铺的面板（或密集排列的木条）和木方架空层组成。常用木板有桉木、柚木、冷杉木、松木等。

旅游区的景园式水景设计要借助水的各种形态效果营造景区氛围。其特点如下表所示：

静水 Still Water	表面无干扰反射体（静面水）	no disturbing refractor on the surface(still water)
	表面有干扰反射体（波纹）	disturbing refractor on the surface(ripples)
	表面有干扰反射体（鱼鳞波）	disturbing refractor on the surface (scale ripples)
垂落 Falling Water	水流速度快的水幕水堰	water curtain and weir with high-speed water flow rate
	水流速度慢的水幕水堰	water curtain and weir with low-speed water flow rate
	间断水流的水幕水堰	water curtain and weir with continual water flow
	动力喷涌、喷射水流	dynamic spout, water gush
流淌 Flowing Water	低流速平滑水墙	smooth water walls with low-speed water flow
	中流速有纹路的水墙	lined water walls with moderate-speed water flow
	低流速水溪、浅池	streams and shallow pools with low-speed water flow
	高流速水溪、浅池	streams and shallow pools with high-speed water flow
跌水 Drop Water	垂直方向瀑布跌水	vertical waterfalls
	不规则台阶状瀑布跌水	irregular step-like waterfalls
	规则台阶状瀑布跌水	regular step-like waterfalls
	阶梯水池	pool with steps
喷涌 Spout	水柱	water column
	水雾	water spray
	水幕	water curtain

(2) Artificial Dynamic Waterscape

A. Waterfall: Waterfall can be divided into various kinds such as Slide Waterfall (Fig.6-16), Step Waterfall (Fig.6-17), Curtain Waterfall (Fig.6-18) and Ribbon Waterfall (Fig.6-19) according to the falling forms. Natural stones or artificial stones, such as landscape stone, distributaries stone, stone to bear falls etc., are

（2）人工动态水景

A. 瀑布跌水：瀑布跌水按其跌落形式分为滑落式（图6-16）、阶梯式（图6-17）、幕布式（图6-18）、丝带式（图6-19）等多种，并模仿自然景观，采用大自然石材或仿石材设置瀑布的背景和引导水的流向（如景石、分

used to imitate natural landscape and guide .

The waterfall will produce different visual and audio effects because of various water flow and volume. As a result, water flow and height become key parameters in the design.

B. Streams: Streams should be reasonably designed according to the environmental conditions, water flow rate, water depth, width and materials. Streams can be divided into 2 styles, Wading and Non-Wading Style(Fig.6-20, Fig.6-21). The wading style is often applied to urban landscape design, whose water depth should be less than 0.3m with non-slip bottom to prevent children from drowning. For non-wading streams, it is suitable to breed some aquatic animals and plants, which adapt to the local climate to enhance the view and interest.

If supported by hills and stones, streams can fully display their natural style. The landscape effects of stone in streams are in the following table:

No	Name	Effect	Position
1	Accent Stone	To form visual focus, bring out the theme and explain name and connotation of the stream	Source or turning point of the stream
2	Isolation Stone	To produce local and trickle sounds	Place where local waterlines change
3	Cut-off Isolation Stone	To diverge and fluctuate the water	To be irregularly arranged in the trickle
4	Wave-cleaving Stone	To diverge the water and make it splash	Streams with sharp slopes and wide water surface
5	Riverbed Stone	To form natural shapes and textures or ornamental stones	Underwater
6	Stepping Stone	To give tourists powerful and stable feelings	To support a large stone
7	Lying Stone	To modulate water flow speed and direction	Places where wide stream turns to narrow and turning point
8	Bottom Stone	To beautify the bottom by planting mosses and algae	Bottom made of pebbles, gravels or ceramic tiles
9	Marking Stone	To decorate water surface and provide convenience for people's walking	To travel through streams and be arranged naturally

流石、承瀑石等）。

瀑布因其水量不同，会产生不同的视觉、听觉效果，因此，落水口的水流量和落水高差的控制成为设计的关键参数。

B. 溪流：溪流的形态应根据环境条件、水量、流速、水深、水面宽和所用材料进行合理的设计。溪流可分为可涉入式（图6-20）和不可涉入式（图6-21）。可涉入式一般常见于城市景观设计中，它的溪流水深应小于0.3米，以防止儿童溺水，同时底部做防滑处理。不可涉入式溪流宜种养适应当地气候条件的水生动植物，增强观赏性和趣味性。

溪流配以山石可充分展现其自然风格，石景在溪流中所起到的景观效果如下表：

序号	名称	效果	应用部位
1	主景石	形成视线焦点、点题、说明溪流名称及内涵	溪流的首位或转向处
2	隔水石	形成局部小落差和细流声响	铺在局部水线变化位置
3	切水石	使水产生分流和波动	不规则布置在细流中间
4	破浪石	使水产生分流和飞溅	用于坡度较大、水面较宽的溪流
5	河床石	观赏石材的自然造型和纹理	设在水面下
6	垫脚石	具有力度感和稳定感	用于支撑大石块
7	横卧石	调节水速和水流方向	溪流宽度变窄和转向处
8	铺底石	美化水底，种植苔藻	多采用卵石、砾石、水刷石、瓷砖铺在基地上
9	踏步石	装点水面、方便步行	横贯溪流、自然布置

C. Ecological Pools: Ecological Pool (Fig.6-22, Fig.6-23) creates an ecological environment of mutual support for animals and plants, not only by offering living place for acoustic plants and animals, but also improving environment and regulating nearby micro-climate. Water is the source of life, so ecological pools can give people and animals a sense of safety, harmony and silence. Well, acoustic animals can bring spirit to waterscape. As a result, acoustic anials are also one of the important factors in the waterscape plan and design.

(3) Swimming–pool Style Waterscape

A. Swimming-Pool: Design of swimming pools in tourist regions must meet the relevant regulations. such Swimming pools should not be designed like those for competitions. Dynamic water can be reached by using beautiful curves as much as possible. According to the function of swimming pools, the designers should design one for children and one for adults or design the two pools as a whole but put the former in a higher position making a water follow across steps or a slope in order to prevent children from falling into adults' swimming pool. Such a design can not only guarantee people's safty but enrich shapes of the swimming pool.

The banks should be designed round and paved with soft infiltration floor or antiskid floor tiles. It will be better to plant various shrubs and trees around swimming pools, provide shade and rest facilities, and set a locker room and picnic equipment if possible(Fig.6-24, Fig.6-25).

B. Artificial Beach: The shallow pool on the artificial beach mainly give people sunbathing experiences. White fine sand is used to cover the bottom of the pool, which forms a gradient slope between 0.2m and 0.6 m from shallow to deep. Its revetment should be made into a gentle slope with stumps to fix the fine sand(Fig.6-26).

(4) Decorative Waterscape

A. Fountains: Fountains totally rely on

C. 生态水池：生态水池（图6-22、图6-23）既适于水下动植物生长，又能美化环境和调节小气候，营造动物和植物互生互养的生态环境。水是生命之源，生态水池给人和动物以安全、和谐、宁静之感，而动物的存在，使水景变得更具有灵性，水生动物也是生态水池规划设计中的要素之一。

（3）泳池式水景

A．游泳池：游泳区域泳池设计必须符合游泳池设计的相关规定。游泳平面不宜作成比赛用池，池边尽可能采用优美的曲线，以加强水的动感。泳池根据功能尽可能分为儿童泳池和成人泳池，也可考虑统一设计，一般将儿童池放在较高的位置，水经阶梯式或斜坡式，避免儿童跌入成人泳池，既保证了安全又可丰富泳池的造型。

池岸必须做圆角处理，铺设软质渗水地面或防滑地砖。泳池周围多种灌木和乔木，并提供休息和遮阳设施，还可设计更衣室和野餐设备（图6-24、图6-25）。

B．人工海滩：人工海滩浅水池主要让人感受日光浴，池底基层上多铺白色细砂，坡度由浅至深，一般为0.2～0.6米之间，驳岸需做成缓坡，以木桩固定细砂（图6-26）。

（4）装饰式水景

A．喷泉：喷泉是完全靠设备

equipment to make waterscape. The key point of fountain design and operation is water jet control. Various patterns can be generated by different jet control and combination.

B. Mirror pool: Interaction between light and water is the essence of waterscape. Mirror pool expands visual space and enriches spatial levels of objects by using inverted reflection of light and shadow on surface of the pool. No matter how small the mirror pool is, it is highly decorative and reflect various objects, such as flowers, grass, trees, elements and rock(Fig.6-27).

The most propriety of mirror pool design is to keep the water in a calm state and avoid disturbance as much as possible. Bottom of the pool should be paved with black or dark green materials (such as black plastic, asphalt clay, black bricks, etc.) to enhance the mirror effect of water.

制造出的水景，对水的射流控制是关键环节，采用不同的手法进行组合，会出现多姿多彩的变化形态。

B. 倒影池：光和水的互相作用是水景景观的精华所在，倒影池正是利用光影在水面形成的倒影，扩大视觉空间，丰富景物的空间层次，增加景观的美感。倒影池极具装饰性，无论水池大小都能产生特殊的借镜效果，花草、树木、小品、岩石前都可置倒影池（图6-27）。

倒影池的设计首先要尽可能避免干扰，保证池水一直处于平静状态。其次是池底要采用黑色和深绿色材料铺装（如黑色塑料、沥青胶泥、黑色砖面等），以增强水的镜面效果。

名称	主要特点	适用场所
壁泉 （图6-28）	由墙壁、石壁和玻璃板上喷出，顺流而下形成水帘和多股水流	广场、居住区入口、景观墙、挡土墙、庭院
涌泉 （图6-29）	水由下向上涌出，泉水柱状，高度 0.6～0.8m 左右，可独立设置也可组成图案	广场、居住区入口、庭院、假山、水池
间歇泉	模拟自然界的地质现象，每隔一定时间喷出水柱和汽柱	溪流、小径、泳池边、假山
旱地喷泉 （图6-30）	将喷泉管道和喷头沉到地面以下，喷水时水流回落到广场硬质铺装上，沿地面坡度排出，平常可作为休闲广场	广场、居住区入口
跳泉 （图6-31）	射流非常光滑稳定，可以稳定准确落在受水孔中，在计算机控制下，生成可变化长度和跳跃时间的水流	庭院、园路边、休闲广场
跳球喷泉	射流呈光滑的水球，水球大小和间歇时间可控制	庭院、园路边、休闲广场
雾化喷泉 （图6-32）	由多组微孔喷管组成，水流通过微孔喷出，看似雾状，多呈雾型和球型	庭院、园路边、休闲广场
喷水盆 （图6-33）	外观呈盆状，下有支柱，可分多级，出水系统简单，多为独立设置	庭院、园路边、休闲广场
小品喷泉 （图6-34）	从雕塑中的器具（罐、盆）和动物（鱼、龙）口中出水，形象有趣	园路边、庭院、休闲场所
组合喷泉 （图6-35）	具有一定规律，喷水形式多样，有层次，有气势，喷射高度高	广场、居住区、入口

Name	Main Features	Application Places
Wall Fountain (Fig. 6-28)	Water gushes out from wall, stone wall or glass board, and forms a water curtain or several currents.	Square, entrance to residential area, landscape wall, retaining wall, and courtyard
Stave Fountain (Fig. 6-29)	Water gushes out from downside up and forms a water column of about 0.6-0.8 m high. Stave can be installed separately or as a group.	Square, entrance to residential area, courtyard, artificial rockwork and pool
Intermittent Fountain	Water gushes out in column or vapor column at intervals, imitating the natural geological phenomenon.	Streams, alleys, swimming pool edge and artificial rockwork
Dry Land Fountain (Fig. 6-30)	The pipelines and fountain heads are placed underground. When water spouts out, it falls onto the pavement of the square and is discharged along the slope of the ground which is used as leisure square in other time.	Square and entrance to residential area
Leap Fountain (Fig. 6-31)	The jet flow is very smooth and stable, and can accurately land in the water hole. The length and jumping time of water flow can be controled by computer.	Courtyard, leisure square and sides of garden road
Jump Ball fountain	The jet flow appears as a smooth water polo, whose size and intermittent time can be controlled.	Courtyard, leisure square and sides of garden road
Spray Fountain (Fig. 6-32)	This type of fountain consists of several groups of pipelines with minor fountain heads. Water gushes out as a mist of fog or ball shape.	Courtyard, leisure square and sides of garden road
Water Basin (Fig. 6-33)	This type usually have a basin and a supporting pillar. The water system is simple and set independently.	Courtyard, leisure square and sides of garden road
Element Fountain (Fig. 6-34)	Water comes out from apparatus (cans, pots) or mouth of an animal(fish, dragon), which is vivid and interesting.	Courtyard, leisure square and sides of garden road
Combination Fountain (Fig. 6-35)	This type has regular patterns. Water spouts out vigorously in various forms and with different levels and has a large jet height.	Square, residential area and entrance

Terms of Landscaping and Gardenning 附 环境景观专业术语

One. Terms of Landscape Architecture	一、园林学常用术语
1. Landscape Architecture	1. 园林学
landscape architecture, garden architecture	园林学
garden making, landscape gardening	造园学
environmental horticulture	环境园艺学
ornamental horticulture	观赏园艺学
garden art, landscape architecture	园林艺术
garden aesthetics, landscape aesthetics	园林美学
garden architecture, landscape architecture	园林建筑学
garden building, landscape hardwork, gartenbau	园林建筑
garden engineering	园林工程
landscape plant	园林植物
ornamental plant	观赏植物
miniature landscape, bonsai, potted landscape，penjing	盆景
garden, park	园林
history of garden architecture	园林学史
garden planning, landscaping planning	园林规划
garden design, landscape design, landscaping	园林设计
gardening machine	园林机具设备
garden management, landscape management	园林管理
landscape ecology	园林生态
greening, planting, afforestation	绿化
environmental greening	环境绿化
green area	绿地面积
ratio of green space	绿地率
urban green coverage	城市绿化覆盖率
factory greening, factory gardening	工厂绿化
street greening, street planting	街道绿化
driveway greening	车行道绿化
drividing stripe greening	分车带绿化
sidewalk greening	人行道绿化
mass planting movement	群众绿化
suburban greening	郊区绿化
highway greening	公路绿化
railway greening, railway planting	铁路绿化
bank planting	堤岸种植
balcony greening	阳台绿化
window-sill greening	窗台绿化
roof greening	屋顶绿化
vertical greening	垂直绿化
climber greening	攀缘绿化
bridgehead greening	桥头绿化
garden	花园
specified flower garden	专类花园
garden village	花园村
landscape garden city	园林城市
rose garden	蔷薇园
conifer garden	松柏园
bulb garden	球根园
perennial garden	宿根园
rock garden, Chinese rockery	假山园
Hunting ground，game area	狩猎场
street crossing center garden	街心花园
petty street garden	小游园
water garden	水景园
paved garden	铺地园
wild plants botanical garden	野趣园

wild plants garden	野生植物园	alpine garden	高山植物园
rustic garden	乡趣园	tropical plants garden	热带植物园
penjing/bonsai garden,miniature landscape	盆景园	medicinal garden, medical plants garden, herb garden	药用植物园
zoo, zoological garden	动物园	green belt/area/space/surface, green open space	绿地
cemetery garden	墓园		
bog and marsh garden	沼泽园	public green space/area	公共绿地
aquatic plants garden	水生植物园	unit green area	单位绿地
school garden	学校园	urban green space	城市绿地
indoor garden	室内花园	street and square green area	街道广场绿地
fragrant garden	芳香花园	residential quarter green area	居住区绿地
garden for the blind	盲人花园	green area\green buffer for environmental protection	防护绿地
park, public park	公园		
city park, urban park	城市公园	suburban green space	郊区绿地
regional park	区公园	residential block green belt	街坊绿地
children's park	儿童公园	attached green space	附属绿地
sports park	体育公园	productive plantation area	生产绿地
forest park	森林公园	nursery	苗圃
memorial park	纪念公园	landscape, scenery, view	风景
martyr memorial park	烈士纪念公园	natural landscape	自然景观
comprehensive park	综合公园	human landscape,scenery of humanities	人文景观
cultural park	文化公园		
cultural and recreation park	文化休憩公园	prairie landscape	草原景观
central park	中央公园	mountain landscape,alpine landscape	山岳景观
natural park, nature park	天然公园		
seaside park,seabeach park, coastal park	海滨公园	geographical landscape	地理景观
		lake landscape, lake view	湖泊景观
historic site park	古迹公园	suburban landscape	郊区景观
riverside park	河滨公园	geological landscape	地质景观
lakeside park	湖滨公园	Karst landscape	喀斯特景观
roadside park, street park	路边公园	vegetative landscape, plants landscape, flora landscape	植物景观
amusement park	娱乐公园		
sculpture park	雕塑公园	2. Ancient Chinese garden	2. 中国古代园林
recreation park	休憩公园		
sanatorium park	疗养公园	classical Chinese garden	中国古典园林
national park	国家公园	traditional Chinese garden	中国传统园林
neighborhood park	邻里公园	ancient Chinese garden	中国古代园林
special park	特种公园	Chinese mountain and water garden	中国山水园
botanical garden, arboretum, vivarium	植物园		
		imperial palace garden	帝王宫苑
abeled plants park	植物公园	royal garden	皇家园林

private garde	私家园林	miniature scenery, abbreviated scenery	缩景
garden on the Yangtze Delta	江南园林	leaking through scenery	漏景
western classical garden	西方古典园林	enframed scenery	框景
maze, labyrinth	迷阵	terminal feature	尾景
Ling You Hunting Garden	灵囿	main feature	主景
Ling Zhao Water Garden	灵沼	secondary feature	副景
term of the Zhou Dynasty	周代术语	objective view	配景
Ling T'ai Platform Garden	灵台	vista line, vista	夹景又称"风景线"
term of the Qin dynasty	秦代术语	foreground	前景
E-Pang Palace	阿房宫	background	背景
Shang-Lin Yuan	上林苑	order of sceneries	景序
term of the Han Dynasty	汉代术语	feature spot, view spot, scenery spot	景点
Wei-Yang Palace	未央宫	garden space	园林空间
Luoyang Palace	洛阳宫	wide open space, wide space	开敞空间
term of Wei Dynasity	魏代术语	enclosed space	封闭空间
Hua-Qing Palace	华清宫	artistic conception, poetic imagery	意境
term of the Tang Dynasty	唐代术语	antiquity	苍古
Gen Yue Imperial Garden	艮岳	spaciousness, airiness	空灵
term of the Song Dynasty	宋代术语	in-motion viewing	动观
The Ruins of Yuanmingyuan/ the Old Summer Palace	圆明园	in-position viewing	静观
Summer Palace	颐和园	axis, axial line	轴线
Chengde Summer Resort	承德避暑山庄	main axis	主轴
Suzhou (traditional) gardens	苏州园林	auxiliary axis	副轴
hanging Garden	悬园又称"悬空园", "架高园"	hidden axis, invisible axis	暗轴又称"隐轴"

3. Garden history of the West　　3. 西方园林史

Royal Botanical Garden, Kew garden	英国皇家植物园又称"邱园"	western classical garden	西方古典园林
Chateau/Palais de Versailles, Versailles Palace	凡尔赛宫苑	English style garden	英国式园林
		Anglo-Chinese style garden	中英混合式园林
Chateau/Palais de Fontainebleau, Fontainebleau Palace	枫丹白露公园	Italian style garden	意大利式园林
view, scenery, feature	景	Spanish style garden	西班牙式园林
distant view	远景	French style garden	法兰西式园林
close shot	近景	Le Notre's style garden	勒诺特尔式园林
obstructive scenery, blocking view	障景又称"抑景"	Renaissance style villa/garden	文艺复兴庄园
		Rococo style garden	洛可式园林
borrowed scenery, view borrowing	借景	Baroque style garden	巴洛克式园林
oppositive scenery, view in opposite place	对景	manor, villa garden, manerlum	庄园
		peristyle garden, patio	廊柱园

Two. Garden art commonly used terms	二、园林艺术常用术语
1. Garden design commonly used terms	1. 园林设计常用术语
upward landscape	仰视景观
downward landscape	俯视景观
seasonal phenomena	季相景观
meteorological diversity	气象景观
scenery	
visual field	视野
autumn scenery	秋色
visual illusion	视错觉
artistic layout of garden	园林艺术布局
symmetrical balance	对称平衡
unsymmetrical balance, unsymmetrical	不对称平衡
bilateral symmetry	左右对称
radial symmetry	辐射对称
perspective line	透景线
Skyline	树冠线
2. Common Terms of Public Leisure Space Planning and Design	2. 公共休闲空间规划设计常用术语
art of garden colors	园林色彩艺术
monochromatic harmony	单色谐调
compound chromatic harmony	复色谐调
contrast colors accent	对比色突出
approximate colors harmony	近似色谐调
warm color	暖色
cool color	冷色
color sensation	色感
urban green space system planning	城市绿地系统规划
green space system	绿地系统
public green space quota	公共绿地定额
public green space norm	公共绿地指标
green space layout	绿地布局
attractive circle	吸引圈
attractive distance	吸引距离
effective radius	有效半径
green space resource	绿地资源

green space effect	绿地效果
planning procedure of green space	绿地规划程序
spatial planning	空间规划
image planning	形象规划
implementary plan	实施规划
necessary living space	必要生活空间
leisure time living space	余暇生活空间
usage frequency	利用频度
planning of trees and shrubs	树种规划
type of green space	绿地类型
annular green space	环状绿地
green plot	块状绿地
green spot	点状绿地
radiate green space	放射状绿地
wedge-shaped green space	楔状绿地
buffer green space	缓冲绿地
noiseproof green space	防音绿地
scientific landscape theory	科学景观论
reserve garden	园林保留地
park planning	公园规划
garden master planning	园林总体规划
site planning	总平面规划
garden zoning	园林分区
tranquil rest area	安静休息区
children playing space	儿童活动区
children playground, playlot, children's play area	儿童游戏场
sports activities area	体育运动区
picnic place	野餐区
pedestrian space	散步区
mass meeting square	群众集会区
ornamental plants area	观赏植物区
display greenhouse area, display Conservatory area	观赏温室区
lawn space	草坪区
shade tree section	绿荫区
historical relics area	历史古迹区
youngsters activities area	青少年活动区
bird sanctuary area	诱鸟区
fishing center	钓鱼区

camp site	野营区	tourism resource	旅游资源
visitors center	游人中心	tourism geography	旅游地理
service center	服务中心	tourism geology	旅游地质
adventure ground	探险游乐场	famous historical city	历史名城
cultural activities area	文化活动区	famous cultural city	文化名城
approach system, road system	道路系统	ashes, ancient cultural relic	文化遗址
circular road system	环形道路系统	natural open museum	天然博物馆
latticed road system	方格形道路系统	natural geomorphology	风景地貌
radiate road system	放射形道路系统	imaginative geomorphologic	造型地貌
informal road system	自然式道路系统	figuration	
formal road system	规整式道路系统	beauty spot, scenic spot, scenic	风景区
mixed style road system	混合式道路系统	area	
garden planning map	园林规划图	place of interest	风景名胜
garden planning direction	园林规划说明书	specific natural scenes area	特异景观风景区
urban park system	城市公园系统	scenic spot of minority customs	民族风俗风景区
distribution of parks	公园分布	alpine scenic spot	高山风景区
park type, park category	公园类型	seabeach scenic spot	海滨风景区
distance between parks	公园间距	forest scenic spot	森林风景区
park styles	公园形式	alpine tundra landscape spot	高山草甸风景区
excursion area, open-to-public	游览区	Valley scenic spot	峡谷风景区
area		river landscape district	江河风景区
No-admittance area	非游览区	lake round scenic spot	湖泊风景区
dministrative area, office area	办公区	hot spring scenic spot	温泉风景区
service center	服务区	waterfall scenic spot	瀑布风景区
dynamic rest space	动休息区	region forbidden to tree	禁伐禁猎区
static rest space	静休息区	cutting and hunting	
entertaining performance	娱乐演出区	region closed for afforestation	封山育林区
place		crater lake scenic spot	天池风景区
main entrance	主要入口	nature protection area, natural	自然保护区
secondary entrance	次要入口	reserve	
visitors flowrate	人流量	protection area for scientific	科学保护区
vehicle flowrate	车流量	research	
park road	公园道路	natural monument	天然纪念物
land-water ratio	公园水陆面积	Biosphere reserve	生物圈保护区
	比率	3. Popular garden plants	3. 常用园林
visitors holding capacity	游人容纳量		植物
landscape resource evaluation	风景资源调查	cumquat, kumquat	金橘
Scenicology	风景学	milan tree	米仔兰(米兰)
landscape plan	风景规划	croton	变叶木
landscape design	风景设计	poinsettia	一品红
tour route	游览路线	chinese hibiscus	扶桑

fringed hibiscus	吊灯花	yew podocarpus	罗汉松
guiana chestnut	马拉巴栗（发财树）	India rubber fig	橡皮树
		smallfruit fig	榕树
camellia	山茶	bougainvillea	叶子花（三角梅）
yunnan camellia	云南山茶	heavenly bamboo	南天竹
golden camellia	金花茶	white michelia	白兰花
daphne	瑞香	banana shrub	含笑
paper bush	结香	creeping rockfoil	虎耳草
fuchsia	倒挂金钟	hydrangeas	八仙花（绣球花）
Japan fatsia	八角金盘	mei flower	梅花
ivy	常春藤	pittosporum	海桐
umbrella tree	鹅掌柴	China green	广东万年青
rhododendron	杜鹃花	monstera ceriman	龟背竹
jasmine	茉莉花	snow flower	苞叶芋
Sweet osmanthus	桂花	spotted dieffenbachia	花叶万年青
oleander	夹竹桃	oyster plant	紫背万年青
lucky-nut-thevetia	黄花夹竹桃	purple heart	紫鸭跖草
frangipani	鸡蛋花	inch plant	吊竹梅
bleeding-heart glorybower	龙吐珠	lily of China	万年青
night jasmine	夜香树（木本夜来香）	aspidistra	蜘蛛抱蛋（一叶兰）
broadleaf raintree	鸳鸯茉莉	asparagus fern	文竹
cape jasmine	栀子花	table fern	凤尾蕨
moth orchid	蝴蝶兰	sword fern	肾蕨
cattleya	卡特兰	venus's-hair-fern	铁线蕨
dendrobium	石斛	bird's-nest fern	鸟巢蕨
lady slipper	兜兰	boston fern	波士顿蕨
orchid	兰花	staghorn fern	鹿角蕨
goering cymbidium	春兰	snake plant	虎尾兰
florists cyclamen	仙客来	agave	龙舌兰
florists gloxinia, common	大岩桐	elephant-foot tree	酒瓶兰
gloxinia		alstroemeria, peruvian lily	六出花
whiplash star of bethlehem	虎眼万年青	hairy fruit musella	地涌金莲
crinum	文殊兰	queen's bird-of-paradise flower	鹤望兰（天堂鸟）
spider lily	蜘蛛兰		
barbadoslily, Amaryllis	朱顶红	shell flower	艳山姜
zephyr lily	葱兰	peacock plant	孔雀肖竹芋
common freesia	香雪兰（小苍兰）	hicolor arrowroot	花叶竹芋
crocus	番红花	clear weed	冷水花
sago cycas	苏铁（铁树）	haby's-breath	锥花丝石竹（满天星）
hoop pine	南洋杉		

royal water lily	王莲	dahlia	大丽花
lotus	荷花	scarlet sage	一串红
water lily	睡莲	pansy	三色堇
picher plant	猪笼草	scarlet kafirlily	君子兰
picher plant	瓶子草	common garden canna，	美人蕉
sundew	茅膏菜	Indian shot	
baby jade	燕子掌	common four o'clock	紫茉莉（地雷花）
mexican snowball	石莲花	chinese pink	石竹
winter pot kalanchoe	长寿花	carnation	香石竹（康乃馨）
oxalis，shamrock，sorrel	红花酢浆草	columbine	耧斗菜
garden nasturtium	旱金莲	clematis	铁线莲
florists flowering begonia	四季秋海棠	herbaceous peony，Chinese	芍药
golden ball	金琥	peony	
sea-wrchin cactus	草球	peony	牡丹
queen of the night	昙花	pulsatilla，windflower	白头翁
orchid cactus	令箭荷花	persian buttercup，crowfoot	花毛茛
oriental moon	绯牡丹	corn poppy	虞美人
right-blooming cereus	量天尺（三棱箭）	bleeding heart	荷包牡丹
crab cactus	蟹爪兰	violet	紫罗兰
periwinkle	长春花	pelargonium	天竺葵
africa violet	非洲紫罗兰	chloranthus	珠兰
golden pachystachys	金苞花	tuberous begonia	球根秋海棠
silvernet plant	网纹草	primrose	报春花
umbrella plant	伞莎草	forget-me-not	勿忘草
flamingo plant,anthurium	花烛	sea lavender，statice	补血草(勿忘我)
giant alocasia	海芋	spearmint	留兰香
common dayflower	鸭跖草	petunia	矮牵牛
chinese aloe	芦荟	mint	薄荷
broadleaf bracket-plant	吊兰	sage	鼠尾草
common orange daylily	萱草	rosemary	迷迭香
common hyacinth	风信子	balloonflower	桔梗
common grape hyacinth	葡萄风信子	transvaal daisy, gerbera	非洲菊(扶郎花)
tulip	郁金香	java velvetplant	紫鹅绒
shorttube lycoris，red spider lily	石蒜	youth-and-old-age，common zinnia	百日草
chinese narcissus	水仙	calla lily	马蹄莲
tuberose	晚香玉	sweet-pea	香豌豆
blackberrylily	射干	common graden coleus	彩叶草
gladiolus，Sword lily	唐菖蒲（剑兰）	molucca balm	贝壳花
iris	鸢尾	slipper wort	蒲包花
daisy	雏菊	florists cineraria	瓜叶菊

peperomia	豆瓣绿	poppy anemone, windflower	欧洲银莲花
roundleaf pilea	镜面草	garland flower, white ginger lily	姜花
snow of June	六月雪		
buddha bamboo	佛肚竹	Chinese wisteria	紫藤
fishtail palm	鱼尾葵	oriental cherry, flowering cherry	樱花
Chinese fan-palm	蒲葵		
palm	棕榈	kudzu	葛藤
lady palm	棕竹	mock strawberry	蛇莓
bottle palm	酒瓶椰子	Chinese flowering crab apple	海棠
parlor palm	袖珍椰子	winter jasmine，forsythia	迎春花
tree of kings	朱蕉	crape myrtle	紫薇
dracaena	龙血树	magnolia	玉兰
marigold	万寿菊	flowering plum	榆叶梅
china aster	翠菊	4. Equipped with common garden plant–sik	4. 常用园林植物配植
top primrose	四季报春		
ross-moss,sun plant	半支莲（松叶牡丹）	Plant arrangement	植物配植
		arrangement of trees and shrubs	树木配植
garden balsam	凤仙花		
common cosmos	波斯菊	group planting, mass planting	群植
common snapdragon	金鱼草	specimen planting, isolated planting	孤植
cockscomb	鸡冠花		
pot marigold	金盏菊	clump planting	丛植
verbena	美女樱	group planting	组植
morning glory	大花牵牛	forest planting	林植
morning glory	茑萝	linear planting	列植
blue phlox	福禄考	opposite planting, coupled planting	对植
ornamental cabbage	羽衣甘蓝		
hollyhock	蜀葵	circular planting	环植
josephs-coat	雁来红	belt planting	带植
cherry redpepper	五色椒	scattered planting, loose planting	散植
common wallflower	桂竹香		
sweet alyssum	香雪球	edge planting	边缘种植
florists chrysanthemus	菊花	boundary planting	边界种植
begonia, Elephant ear	秋海棠	architectural planting	整形种植
lily	百合	foundation planting	基础种植
crown imperial	花贝母	corner planting	角隅种植
lovely gloriosa	嘉兰	planting as enframent	景框种植
bulbous iris	球根鸢尾	guard planting	门卫种植
snowdrop	雪花莲（雪钟花）	fence planting	篱恒种植
rainflower	韭莲	screen planting	障景种植
gayfeather，Blazing star	蛇鞭菊	background planting	背景种植

underwood planting	林下种植	paved bed	铺石花坛
roadside planting	路边种植	shrub bed	灌木花坛
hedge	绿篱	parterre	图案花坛群
espalier	树墙	herbaceous flower bed	草药花坛
shade tree	庭荫树	knot bed	花结花坛
specimen tree	园景树	formal flower bed	整形花坛
amenity forest, ornamental	风景林	flower border	花境
forest		flower tub	花桶
avenue tree, street tree	行道树	planting box	植树箱
memorial forest	纪念林	movable flower bed	活动花坛
topiary tree	整型树	5. Landscape and	5. 园林景观及
flower hedge	花篱	Architecture	建筑
thorny plants hedge	刺篱	landscape architect, garden	园林设计师
evergreen hedge	常绿绿篱	designer	
deciduous hedge	落叶绿篱	garden site survey map	园址测量图
high hedge	高篱	topographic map, contour map	地形图
hah-hah fence	沟中边篱	planting design	种植设计
pattern dwarf hedge	图案矮篱	topographical reform design	地形改造设计
labyrinth hedge	迷宫绿篱	detail planting design	种植大样图
clipped hedge	整剪绿篱	cost analysis	造价分析
natural flowering hedge	自然式花篱	garden style	园林形式
boundary fence	边篱	formal garden style	规整式园林
garden fence, garden hedge	园篱	informal garden style	非规整园林
pure forest	纯林	geometric garden style	几何式园林
mixed forest	混交林	natural garden style	自然式园林
open space in woodland	林间隙地	mixed garden style	混合式园林
spinney	杂木林	Modern Baroque style	近代巴洛克式
tree canopy	树冠覆盖面		园林
lawn	草坪	Marx abstract garden	马克斯抽象园林
formal lawn	整形草坪	garden area division	园林区划
flowering lawn	开花草坪	garden block planning	园林分区规划
meadowy land	牧场草坪	courtyard garden	庭院花园
flower bed	花坛	front yard, forecourt	前庭
roadside flower bed	路边花坛	back yard, rear yard	后庭
ribbon flower bed	带状花坛	patio	中庭
flower clock	时钟花坛	kitchen yard	厨园
potted flower bed, basined	盆栽花坛	sunken garden	沉[床]园
flower bed		window garden	窗园
raised flower bed	高设花台	wall garden	墙园
carpet bed	毛毡花坛	home garden	宅园
mosaic bed	镶嵌花坛	terrace garden	台地园

winter garden	冬园	pool	水池
cut flower garden	切花园	pond	水塘
roof garden	屋顶花园	fountain	喷泉
back yard garden	后花园	fountain pool	喷水池
topographical reform of garden	园林地形改造	wading pool	涉水池
earth piled hill, artificial mound	土山	mirror pool, reflecting pool	倒影池
		water-lily pool	睡莲池
rockery, artificial rockwork	假山	piping schema	喷水管布置
Taihu stone, water modelled stone	太湖石	fishing pond	钓鱼塘
		high water table pond	高水位池塘
yellowish brown stone	黄石	seat wall surrounded pool	池边坐人矮墙
artificial stone, man-made stone	人造假山石	secret fountain	隐头喷泉
		island garden	岛园
monolith, standing stone	孤赏石	peninsula garden	半岛园
piled stone hill, hill making	掇山	isle	小岛
stones laying	叠石	waterfall	瀑布
flag stone	板石	cascade	小瀑布
scattered stone	散点石	lake	湖
corner stone	抱角石	rock projecting over water	矶
foundation stone	屋基石	water curtain cave	水帘洞
guard stone	排衙石	garden bridge	园桥
screen stone	屏石	arch bridge	拱桥
rock bank	石岸	stone slab bridge	石板桥
stone steps	石阶	plank bridge	木板桥
stepping stone on water surface	汀步	log bridge	圆木桥
stone appended to wall	附壁石	pavilion bridge	亭桥
stone flower bed	石花台	zigzag bridge	曲桥
stone bench	石凳	wall fountain	壁泉
rock retaining wall	假山石挡土墙	drinking fountain	饮水喷头
dry stone wall	干砌石	garden vase	瓶饰
rock stairway	假山石楼梯	shrub border	灌木花境
stone pavilion	石亭	mixed border	混合花境
stone cavern	石洞	garden road design, garden path design	园林道路设计
grotto	石窟		
stone arrangement, stone layout	置石	trail, footway	漫步路
		alley, path	小径
arch stone	拱石	lawn island	川草坪岛
key stone	拱顶石	safety island	安全岛
water scenes of garden	园林水景	turning curvature	转弯曲度
water body	水体	turning radius	转弯半径
water surface	水面	landing pitch	踏面

stepping stone	步石	new-moon pool	月池
wading step	涉水踏步	small garden ornaments	园林小品
crazy paving path	错铺路	painted tile mural tablet	磁砖壁画
flag stone path paved at	随意组合方石	garden chair, garden seat	园椅
random	板路	garden bench	园凳
pattern path	花纹路	garden table	园桌
mall, avenue	林荫路	garden lamp	园灯
boulevard	林荫大道	sundial	日规
parkway	花园路	bird bath	鸟浴
path in woodland	林间小道	bird cottage, nestle box	鸟舍
planting bed	种植池	bird cage, bird coop	鸟笼
tree grate	树池保护格栅	hanging basket	悬篮
tree guard	树干保护套栏	bird feeder	野鸟喂食器
seatwall-surrounded planting	树池坐凳矮墙	horizontal inscribed board	额匾
score line	路面线纹	couplet written on scroll,	楹联
traditional garden building	传统园林建筑	couplet on pillar	
summer shelter	凉亭	open barbecue	引露天烤炉
arbor, tent arbor	活树亭	living-tree pergola	树棚
mushroom pavilion	蘑菇亭	pergola	花架
thatched pavilion	茅亭	trellis, treillage	花格架
bamboo pavilion	竹亭	naming pailou, decorated	点景牌楼
tea booth, tea kiosk	茶亭	archway	
cloister	回廊	garden layout, garden	园林施工
corridor on water	水廊	construction	
zigzag veranda	曲廊	planting engineering	种植工程
sloping gallery	扒山廊	big tree transplanting	大树移植
two-storied gallery	楼廊	bare root transplanting	裸根移植
painted pleasure boat	画舫	ball transplanting	土球移植
stone boat	石舫	trench planting	沟植
immovable pleasure boat	不击舟	heeling in, temporary planting	假植
poem-engraved stone slab	诗条石	seeding lawn	播种草坪
moon gate	月洞门	sodding lawn	铺草皮块草坪
handrail	扶手栏杆	rockery engineering	假山工程
seat rail	坐凳栏杆	five methods" of rock piling	掇山五法
stone tablet, stele	石碑	method of making the rock	等分平衡法
open garden theater	园林露天剧场	equa-tional and balanced	
open garden dancing place	园林露天舞池	method of making the front	前轻后重法
outdoor music stand	露天音乐台	part of rock lighter than the	
prospect deck	眺望台	back part	
plant propagation greenhouse	繁殖温室	method of lowering the center	上轻下重法
public conservatory	展览温室	of ravity of rocks	

method of unifying the rock veins	纹理统一法	twiner, twinning plant	缠绕植物
method of unifying the rock mate-rials	石料统一法	coniferals	针叶植物
ornamental tree and shrub	观赏树木	broad-leaved plant	阔叶植物
foliage plant	观叶植物	variegate-leaved plant	斑叶植物
fruit-effect plant	观果植物	conifer	松柏植物
plants with ornamental trunks and branches	观枝干植物	evergreen plant	常绿植物
		semi-evergreen plant	半常绿植物
indicating plant	指示植物	non-hardy plant	不耐寒植物
accent plant	主景植物	half-hardy plant	半耐寒植物
damp tolerant plant	耐湿植物	hardy plant	耐寒植物
wind-resistant plant	抗风植物	drought enduring plant	耐旱植物
saline-alkali tolerant plant	耐盐碱植物	stone material	山石材料
city flower	市花	Kunshan stone	昆山石
city tree	市树	stalactite	钟乳石
national flower	国花	Lingbi stone	灵壁石
national tree	国树	Yingde stone	英德石
fragrant plant	芳香植物	Qing stone	青石
pollution resistant plant	抗污染植物	Xuan stone	宣石
environment protecting plant	环保植物	Fangshan stone	房山石
alpine plant	高山植物	ornamental animal	观赏动物
rock plant	岩生植物	ornamental bird	观赏鸟类
climbing plant, climber	攀援植物	ornamental beast	观赏兽类
ground cover plant	地被植物	ornamental insect	观赏昆虫类
shade plant	阴生植物		

6. Garden machinery and equipment — 6. 园林机具设备

decorative plant	装饰植物	garden machine	园林机械
edging plant	装缘植物	garden instrument, garden implement	园林工具
hedge plant	绿篱植物	garden equipment	园林设备
lawn plant, lawn grass	草坪植物	plastic bed divider	花坛分界隔板
bedding plant	花坛植物	planting container	种植容器
bulbous plant	球根植物	log peg	圆木桩
perennial plant, perennial	宿根植物	jet bubbler	喷射装置
aquatic plant, hydrophyte	水生植物	drip irrigator, trickle irrigator	滴灌
xerophyte	旱生植物	circle sprinkler	环动喷灌器
bog plant, swamp plant	沼泽植物	rotor sprinkler	圆筒喷灌器
indoor decorative plant, house plant	室内装饰植物	automatic controller	自控器
		hose end sprinkler	管端喷灌器
cut flower	切花	stationary sprinkler	固定喷灌器
pendulous plant, weeping plant	垂枝植物	mist sprinkler, spray head sprinkler	喷雾喷灌器

sprinkler coverage	喷灌覆盖面	pot watering system	盆栽灌水系统
lawn feeder	草坪加肥器	greenhouse climate controller	温室气候控制器
combined feeder and sprinkler	施肥喷灌器	greenhouse covering	温室覆盖
liquid fertilizer mixer-proportioner	液肥混合调配器	automatic mist control system	喷雾自控系统
		CO_2 generator	二氧化碳发生器
emitter, dripper	滴水喷头	temperature alarm	温度报警钟
erosion control plastic net	水土保持塑料网	tourist car	游览车
nursery stock package material	苗木包装材料	lawn mower	剪草机
		power lawnmower	动力剪草机
burlap bag	麻布袋	horse lawnmower	畜力剪草机
wire basket	铁丝篮	hand lawnmower	手推剪草机
basket container	篮状种植器	visitors investigation	游人调查
plastic nurserican	塑料苗木桶	visitors statistics	游人统计
seed tray	播种盘	garden visitors analysis	游人分析
mesh pot	网孔盆	visitors management	游人管理
fertile peat pot	含肥泥炭盆	tourist map	导游图
potting machine	盆栽机	tour description and direction	导游解说
repotting machine	换盆机	labour management	劳动管理
reclaimed paper container	再生纸种植器	material handling, goods handling	物资管理
wood fiber plant grower	纤维育苗器	equipment management, facility management	设备管理
peat seeding pellet, peat seeding starter	泥炭压制播种饼	financial management	财务管理
cultivator	松土除草机	safety management	安全管理
rotary hoe	旋转锄	environmental monitoring	环境监测
foliage cutter	切叶机	plant maintenance and management	植物养护管理
uncovering plough	翻地犁	garden technical management	园林技术管理
mounted spreader	盖土机	quality management	质量管理
front mounted loader	前悬装土机	garden feature maintenance	园貌维修
rear mounted loader	后缀装土机	plant trimming and pruning	植物整形修剪
spindle mower	旋轴剪草机	disease and insect control	植物病虫防治
planting machine	栽植机	management plan	园林管理规划
plant mulching	植物覆盖	treatment of visitors opinions	游人意见处理
mulch spreader	覆盖物分散机	visitors regulation	游人规则
hydro seeder	种子液肥喷洒机	traffic control in park	园内交通管理
pruning shear	修枝剪	traffic control out of park entrance	园外交通管理
garden seeder	播种器	parking rules	汽车停车规则
bulb planter	球根种植器	bicycle parking rules	自行车停放规则
pH-value computer	土壤酸度探测器	opening hours	开放时间
fertilizer analyzer	肥效分析器		
grafting knife	嫁接刀		
greenhouse equipment	温室设备		

daily sanitation and hygiene management	日常清洁卫生管理	garden microclimate	园林小气候
human ecological environment	人类生态环境	environmental conservation plant	环境保护植物
natural system	自然系统	climatic regulation	引气候调节
natural resource	自然资源	homeostasis	自动调节机能
conservation of nature	自然保护	ecological equilibrium/balance	生态平衡
nature preservation	自然保存	forest ecosystem	森林生态系统
environmental protection	环境保护	prairie/grassland ecosystem	草原生态系统
environment capacity	环境容量	dust holding plant	滞尘植物
environment fitness	环境适宜性		
ambient air quality	环境空气质量标准	**Three. Terms of Construction History**	**三、建筑史相关专业术语**
symbiosis	共生		
mutualism	互惠共生	1. Ancient Chinese Architecture	1. 中国古代建筑相关
public nuisance	公害	Ancient Chinese Architecture and Construction	中国古代建筑及构造
ecocide	生态绝灭	palace,temple	宫
ecosystem	生态系统	hall	殿
ecosphere	生态圈	hall	厅又称"堂"
ecological disaster	生态灾难	room	室
environmental quality	环境质量	house	房
environment stress	环境压力	pavilion	亭
life-support system	生命维持系统	platform	台
feedback system	反馈系统	altar	坛
autotroph	自养生物	storied building	楼
heterotroph	异养生物	pavilion	阁
foodchain	食物链	colonnade	廊
biosphere	生物圈	pavilion on terrace	榭
endangered/threatened plant	濒危植物	waterside pavilion	水榭
major community	主体群落	windowed veranda	轩
artificial community	人工群落	folk house	民居
green revolution	绿色革命	quadrangle	四合院
outdoor recreation resource	户外娱乐资源	stockaded village	寨
wilderness environment system	原始环境系统	boat house	舫
modern environment system	近代环境系统	que, watchtower	阙
country life-pattern	乡村生活模式	pailou, decorated gateway	牌楼
smoke damage, fume damage	烟害	huabiao, ornamental pillar	华表
fog damage	雾害	pagoda	塔
frost injury	霜害	flush gable roof	硬山
water pollution	水污染	overhanging gable roof	悬山
soil pollution, soil contamination	土壤污染		

gable and hip roof	歇山	3-purlin beam	三架梁
hip roof	庑殿	flat-topped beam, 3-purlin beam	平梁
hip roof	四阿	4-purlin beam	四架梁
round ridge roof	卷棚	5-purlin beam	五架梁
double eaves	重檐	5-purlin beam	四椽栿
pyramidal roof	攒尖	6-purlin beam	六架梁
round pavilion roof	圆攒尖	7-purlin beam	七架梁
wooden structure	大木	7-purlin beam	六椽栿
wooden frame with dougong	大式	9-purlin beam	九架梁
wooden frame without dougong	小式	9-purlin beam	八椽栿
carpentry work	大木作	one-step cross beam	单步梁
joinery work	小木作	two-step cross beam	双步梁
post and lintel construction	抬梁式构架	main aisle exposed tiebeam	挑尖梁
column and tie construction	穿斗式构架	rufu, beam tie	乳栿
log cabin construction	井干式构架	baotou beam	抱头梁
peripheral column	檐柱	penetrating tie	穿插枋
principle column, Hypostyle column	金柱	cantilevered corner beam, hip rafer	角梁
hypostyle column	内槽柱	purlin (used with dougong)	木行大式
interior column	内柱	purlin (used without dougong)	檩小式
gable column, center column	山柱	purlin	抟
corner column	角柱	ridged purlin	脊（木行）大式
short column	瓜柱	ridged purlin	脊檩小式
king post	脊瓜柱	ridged purlin	脊抟
king post	蜀柱	intermediate purlin	金（木行）大式
suspended column	雷公柱	intermediate purlin	金檩小式
suspended column	帐杆	intermediate purlin	上中平抟
Cejiao	侧脚	purlin on hypostyle	老檐（木行）大、小式
entasis treatment	卷杀		
shuttle-shaped column	梭柱	eave purlin	正心（木行大式）
bracket	角背	eave purlin	檐檩小式
inverted V-shaped brace	由戗	eave purlin	下平抟
chashou, inverted V-shaped brace	叉手	architrave(used with dougong)	额枋大式
		architrave(used with dougong)	檐枋小式
wooden pier	柁墩	architrave	阑额
tuofeng, camel-hump shaped	驼峰	terms of the Song Dynasty	宋代术语
suport		cushion board	由额垫板大式
beam	梁	cushion board	檐垫板小式
beam	栿	tiebeam	枋
crescent beam	月梁	ridge tiebeam	脊枋

環境藝術設計專業英語教程

upper purlin tiebeam	上金枋	niche	龛
lower purlin tiebeam	下金枋	antique shelf	博古架
eave tiebeam	老檐枋大式，指檐口构造	masonry	瓦石作
		eave wall	檐墙
eave tiebeam	檐枋小式，指檐口构造	partition wall	廊墙
		horizontal partition wall	扇面墙
top rafter	顶椽	vertical partition wall	隔断墙
upper rafter	脑椽	sill wall	槛墙
intermediate rafter	花架椽	gable wall head	犀头
eave rafter	檐椽	cantilever stone on eave	挑檐石
flying rafter	飞檐椽	stepped gable wall	五花山墙
flying rafter	飞子	corbel, hanging over	拔檐
eave edging	连檐	corbel, hanging over	叠涩
tile edging	瓦口	corner pier	角柱石
tile edging	额版	rectangular stone slab	阶条石
raising-of-truss method; raising the purlin	举架	rectangular stone slab	压阑石
		steps	台阶、踏步
raising the purlin	举析	intermediate pier	斗板石
horizontal spacing between purlins	步架	drooping belt stone	垂带
		drooping belt stone	副子
cai	材	triangular space	象眼
partition door	格栅	Yulu, imperial path	御路
window stool	抹头	ramp	羌差
grill	棂子	xumizuo	须弥座
panel	裙板	guijiao	圭角
sill wall window	槛窗	upper fillet and fascia	上枋
window sill	榻板	lower fillet and fascia	下枋
removable window	支摘窗	upper cyma, recta	上袅
door bearing	门枕	lower cyma, reversa	下袅
decorative cylinder	门簪	suyao	束腰
door knocker	门跋	balustrade	钩栏
decorative nails on door leaf	门钉	single frieze balustrade	单钩栏
bearing stone	门枕石	double frieze balustrade	垂台钩栏
drum-shaped bearing stone	抱鼓石	baluster	望柱
ceiling	天花	baluster capital	望柱头
lattice framing	帽儿梁	frieze panel	栏版
lattice framing	支条	frieze panel	华版
compartment ceiling	井口天花	plinth stone	地伏
flat ceiling	海墁天花	handrail	寻杖
caisson ceiling	藻井	pedestal boulder, capital stone	柱顶石
shelf	罩	column base	柱础

zhi	趾	central nave	中厅
stone tablet	碑碣	aisle	侧廊
2. Ancient Foreign Architecture	2. 外国古代建筑相关	apse	半圆形壁龛
		transept	袖廊
pyramid	金字塔	colonnade	柱廊
obelisk	方尖碑	altar	神坛
pylon	牌门楼	arcade	拱廊
lotus column	莲花式柱	blind arcade	壁上拱廊
papyrus column	纸草花式柱	turret	塔楼
palm column	棕榈叶式柱	rose window	玫瑰窗
ziggurat	塔庙	buttress	扶壁
peristyle	列柱围廊式	pinnacle	尖顶
pediment	山花	gargoyle	滴水兽
doricorder	多立克柱式	finial	顶端饰
ionic order	伊奥尼亚柱式,曾用名"爱奥尼亚柱式"。	tracery	花色窗棂
		quatrefoil	四叶饰
		cinquefoil	五叶饰
corinthian order	科林斯柱式	mansion,palazzo	府邸
cornice	檐口	drum	鼓座
entablature	檐部	lantern	采光塔
frieze	檐壁	bulleye window	小侧窗
architrave	额枋	cartouche, scroll work	涡卷装饰
capital	柱头	minaret	宣礼塔
column shaft	柱身	mihrab, prayer niche	圣龛
flute	沟	mimbar, pulpit	肋骨拱
torus	圆底线脚	vault type	星形拱
plinth	柱基	barrel vault	网状拱
stylobate	台基	groin vault	扇形拱
aqueduct	输水道	rib bed vault	讲坛
Pantheon	万神庙	stellar vault	拱式
triumphal arch	凯旋门	reticulated vault	简拱
colosseum	角斗场	fan vault	棱拱
forum	广场	trough vault	倒槽式拱
Tuscan order	托斯卡柱式	stalactite vault	钟乳拱
potch, portico	门廊	arch type	拱式
cupola	小穹顶	semicircular arch	半圆拱
reglet	平嵌线	pointed arch	尖拱
main dome	主穹顶	segmental arch	弧形拱
semi dome	半穹顶	ogee arch	葱花拱
pendentive	帆拱	horseshoe arch	马蹄拱
basilica	会堂	squinch	交角拱

dome type	穹式	Group	分组菜单
semespherical dome	半球形穹顶	Mirror	镜像
ogee dome	葱花穹顶	Group	分组
square dome	方穹顶	Array	阵列
arabesque	阿拉伯花饰	Open	打开
Arabian capital	阿拉伯式柱头	Align	对齐
		Close	关闭

Four. Terminology commonly used design software

四、常用设计软件专业术语

		Place Highlight	放置高亮区
1. 3D	1. 3D	Ungroup	解除群组
3DMAX of a bilingual	3DMAX的中英文对照	Align Camera	对齐摄像机
		Explode	分解
File	文件	Scaping Tool	间距修改工具
Edit	编辑	Detach	分离
Rest	重置	Transform Type-In	输入变换坐标
Undo	撤消	Attach	合并
Save Selected	保存所选择的对象	isplay Floater	显示浮动物体
Redo	恢复	Hide	隐藏
Xref Objects	外部参考物体	Freeze	冻结
Clone	复制	Selection Floater	选择浮动物体
Xref Scenes	外部参考场景	Snapshot	快照复制
Delete	删除	Normal Align	法向对齐
Merge	合并	Material Editor	材质编辑器
Select All	对象选择	Material/Map Browser	材质/贴图浏览器
Replace	替换	VIEWS	视图菜单
Select None	取消对象	Undo Redo	撤消重复
Import	输入	Save Active View	保存当前激活的视图状态
Select Invert	对象反转	Restore Active View	还原当前激活的视图状态
Export Hold	输出保存		
Archive	压缩存盘	Grids	栅格
Fetch	取出	Show Home Grid	显示主栅格
View File	观看文件	Activate Home Grid	激活主栅格
Select BY	根据选择	Activate Grid Object	激活栅格对象
Select By Color)	根据颜色选择	ALign To View	对齐视图
Select By Name	根据名字.选择	Viewport Background	背景图像
Region	区域	Update Background	更新背景图像
Edit Named Selections	编辑已命名被选物	Transform	
		Rest Background Transform	重设背景转换
Properties	属性	Show Transform Gizmo	显示转换范围框
Tools	工具菜单	Show Ghosting	显示前后帖
		Show Key Times	显示轨迹点时间

Shade selected	阴影选择	Instance	关联复制
Show Dependencies	显示从属物体	Edit Stack	编辑堆栈对话框
Instances	相依物体	Reference	参考复制
Reference	参考物体	Material Editor	材质编辑器
Match Camera To View	相机与视图相配	Reglection	反射
Add Default Lights To Scene	向场景添加缺省	Basic Parameters	基本参数
	灯光	Refraction	折射
Redraw All Views	重画所有的视图	Ambient	环境反射
Deactivate All Maps	休眠所有贴图	3D Procedural Maps	三维贴图
Update During Spinner Drag	微调控制项拖动	Diffuse	漫反射
	时更新	Face-mapped	面贴图
Expert Mode	专家模式	Specular	镜面反射
Object	物体工具栏	Extended Parameters	扩展参数
Create	创建命令面板	Maps	贴图
Compounds	复合工具栏	Bitmap	位图
Modify	修改命令面板	Checker	棋盘格
Lighes&Cameras	光线和照相机工	Composite materials	复合材质
	具栏	Gradient	渐变
Hierarchy	层级命令面板	Double Sided	双面
Particles	粒子系统工具栏	Adobe Photoshop Plug-In	PS滤镜
Motion	运动命令面板	Filter	
Helpers	帮助物体工具栏	Blend	混合
Display	显示命令面板	Adove Premiere Video Filter	PM滤镜
Space Warps	空间扭曲工具栏	Matte/Shoadow	磨砂
Utilities	实用程序	Cellular	细胞
Modifiers	修改工具栏	Multi/Sub-object	多重子物体
Rendering	渲染工具栏	Dent Raytrace	凹痕光线追踪
Shapes	二维图形工具栏	Noise	干扰
Modeling	造型修改工具栏	Top/Bottom	项底
Modifier Stack	编辑修改器堆栈	Splat	油彩
Cloning and Boolean Object	布尔运算与克隆	Matrble	大理石
	对象	Wood	木纹
Pin Stack	钉住堆栈状态	Water	水
Union	并集	Time Configuration	时间帧速率
Active/Inactive	激活/不激活切换	Falloff	衰减
Subtraction	差集	Frame Rate	帧速率
Show End Result	显示最后结果	Flat Mirror	镜面反射
Intersection	交集	NTSC	NTSC制式
Make Unipue	使独立	Mask	罩框
Copy	复制	Film	胶片速度
Remove Modifier	删除编辑修改器	Mix	混合

PAL	PAL制式	Teeter	轴向变形
Output	输出	Geosphere	经纬球
Custom	自定义	Bevel	倒角
Planet	行星	Cylinder	柱体
Raytrace	光线跟踪	Fit	适配变形
Reglect/Refrace	反射/折射	Tube	管子
Smoke	烟雾	Torus	圆环
Create	创建	Pyramid	金字塔
Speckle	斑纹	Teapot	茶壶
Helpers	帮助物体	Plane	平面
Stucco	泥灰	District parameters Volume column Show	参数区卷展栏
Dummy	虚拟体		
Vertex Color	项点颜色	Shader Basic Parameters	着色基本参数区
Forward Kinematics	正向运动	Blinn	宾氏
Composite	合成贴图	Anisotropic	各向异性
Inverse Kinematics	反向运动	Metal	金属
Particle age	粒子寿命	Multi-layer	多层式
Patticle Mblur	粒子模糊	Phong	方氏
Control equipment of the type of two-dimensional point	控制器械的种类 二维项点	Oren-Nayar-Blinn	表面粗糙的对象
		Strauss	具有简单的光影
Track View	轨迹视图		分界线
Smooth	光滑项点	Wire	线架结构显示
Assign Controller	指定控制器		模式
Corner	边角项点	2-Sided	双面材质显示
Replace Controller	替换控制器	Face Map	将材质赋予对象
Bezier	Bezier项点		所有的面
Linear Controller	直线控制器	Faceted	将材质以面的形
Bezier Corner	Bezier角点		式赋予对象
TCB Contriller	TCB控制器	Blinn Basic Patameters	宾氏基本参数区
Contriller	连续	Diffuse	固有色
Path Controller	路径控制器	Ambient	阴影色
List Controller	列表控制器	Specular	高光色
Expression Controller	噪声控制器	Self-Illumination	自发光
Look At	看着	Opacity	不透明度
Three-dimensional modeling	三维造型	Specular Highlights	高光曲线区
Deformations	变形控制	Specular Level	高光级别
Box	盒子,立方体	Glossiness	光泽度
Scale	缩放	Soften	柔和度
Cone	圆锥体	Extended Parameters	扩展参数区
Twist	扭曲	Falloff	衰减
Sphere	球体	Filer	过滤法

Subtractive	删减法	Cellular	细胞
Additive	递增法	Matte/Shadow	投影材质
Index of Refraction	折射率	Checker	棋盘格
Wire	线架材质	Matte	不可见
Reflection Dimming	反射暗淡	Composite	合成贴图
SuperSampling	超级样本	Atmosphere	大气
Maps	贴图区	Dent	凹痕贴图
Ambient Color	阴影色贴图	Apply Atmosphere	加入大气环境
Diffuse Color	固有色贴图	Falloff	衰减
Specular Color	高光色贴图	At Background Depth	在背景深度
Glossiness	光泽度贴图	Flat Mirror	镜面反射
Self-Illmination	自发光贴图	At Object Depth	在物体深度
Opacity	不透明贴图	Gradient	渐变
Filter Color	过滤色贴图	Shadow	阴影
Bump	凹凸贴图	Marble	大理石
Reflction	反射贴图	Receive Shadow	接受阴影
Refraction	折射贴图	Madk	罩框
Refract Map/Ray Trace IOR	折射贴图/光线	Shadow Brightness	阴影的亮度
	跟踪折射率	Mix	混合
Displacement	置换贴图	Reflection	反射
Dvnamics Properties	动力学属性区	Noise	干扰
The type of material	材质类型	Morpher	形态结构贴图
Blend	混合材质	Output	输出
Material#1	材质#1	Muti/Sub-Object	多重子物体材质
Material#2	材质#2	Partcle Age	粒子寿命
Mask	屏蔽	Set Number	设置数目
Interactive	交互	Perlin Marble	珍珠岩
Mix Amount	混合数值	Number Of Materials	材质数目
Mixing Curve	混合曲线	Planet	行星
Use Curve	使用曲线	Raytrace	光线追踪材质
Transition Zone	交换区域	Raytrance	光线跟踪
Composite	合成材质	Shading	明暗
Composite Bisic Parameters	合成材质基础参	Reflect/Refract	反射/折射
	数区	2-Sided	双面
Base Material	基本材质	RGB Multiply	RGB倍增
Mat.1～Mat.9	材质1～材质9	Face Map	面贴图
Double Sided	双面材质	RGB Tint)	RGB染色
Translucency	半透明贴图类型	Wire	线框
Facing material	表面材质	Smoke	烟雾
Bitmap	位图	Super Sample	超级样本
Back Material	背面材质	Speckle	斑纹

Ambient	阴影色	Show Core	显示视域范围
Splat	油彩	Shadow Map Params	阴影贴图参数
Diffuse	固有色	Show Horizor	显示地平线
Stucco	泥灰	Target Spot	目标聚光灯
Reflect	反射	Near Range	最近范围
Thin Wall Refraction	薄壁折射	Free SPot	自由聚光灯
Luminosity	发亮度	Far Range	最远范围
Vertex Color	顶点颜色	Target Direct	目标平行光灯
Transparency	透明	Render Scene)	渲染
Water	水	Rime Output	输出时间
Index Of Refr	折射率	Single	渲染单帖
Wood	木纹	Range	所有帖
Specular Highlight	反射高光	Output Size	输出尺寸
Specular Color	高光反射颜色	Rendering)	渲染
Shininess	反射	Environment	环境粒子系统
Shiness Strength	反光强度	Background	背景
Environment	环境贴图	Spray	喷射
Bump	凹凸贴图	Global Lighting	球形照明
Shellac	虫漆材质	Snow	雪
Base Material	基础材质	Atmosphere	大气
Shellac Material	虫漆材质	Blizzard	暴风雪
Shellac Color Blend	虫漆颜色混合	Combustion	燃烧
Standard	标准材质	PArray	粒子列阵
Top/Bottom	顶/底材质	Volume Light	体光
Top Material	顶材质	Pcloud	粒子云
Bottom Material	底材质	Fog	雾
Swap	置换	Super Spray	超级喷射
Coordinates	坐标轴	Standard	标准
Blend	融合	Layered	分层
Possition	状态	Volume Fog)	体雾
The type of light camera type	灯光类型 摄像机类型	**2. CAD of a bilingual**	**2. CAD的中英文对照**
Omni	泛光灯	2D Solid	二维实体 2D实面
Target	目标	2D Wireframe	二维线框
General Parameters	普通参数	3D Array	三维阵列 3D 阵列
Lens	镜头尺寸	3D Dynamic View	三维动态观察 3D 动态检视
Projector Parameters	投射贴图		
FOV	视域范围	3D objects	三维物体 3D 物件
Attenuation Parameters	衰减参数	3D Orbit	三维轨道 3D 动态
Stock Lenses	镜头类型	3D Orbit	三维动态观察 3D 动态
Shadow Parameters	阴影参数		

附 环境景观专业术语

3D Studio	3D工作室（软件）	Administration dialog box	管理对话框 管理对话方块
3D Viewpoint	三维视点 3D 检视点	Advanced Setup Wizard	高级设置向导 进阶安装精灵
3dpoly	三维多段线 3D 聚合线	Aerial View	鸟瞰视图 鸟瞰视景
3dsin 3DS	3DS 输入 3D 实体汇入	Affine calibration	仿射校准 关系校正
3DSolid	三维实体 3D 实体	Alert	警告 警示
3dsout 3DS	输出 3D 实体汇出	Alias	别名
Abort	放弃 中断	Aliasing	走样 锯齿化
Abort	中断 中断	Align	对齐
Absolute coordinates	绝对坐标 绝对座标	Aligned dimension	对齐标注 对齐式标注
Abut	邻接 相邻	Alignment	对齐(方式) 对齐
Accelerator key	加速键 快速键	Allocate	分配 配置
Access	获取 存取	Altitude	标高 高度
Acisin ACIS	ACIS输入 ACIS 汇入	Ambient color	环境色 环境颜色
		Ambient light	环境光 环境光源
Acisout ACIS	ACIS输出 ACIS 汇出	Angular dimension	角度标注
		Angular unit	角度单位
Action	操作 动作	Annotation	注释
Active	活动（的）作用中	Anonymous block	无名块 匿名图块
Adaptive sampling	自适应采样 最适取样	Anti-aliasing	反走样 消除锯齿
		Aperture	靶框 锁点框
Add	添加 加入	Apparent intersections	外观交点 外观交点
Add a Printer	添加打印机 新增印表机	Append	附加 附加
		Application key	授权申请号 应用程式码
Add mode	添加模式		
Add Plot Style Table	添加打印样式表	Appload	加载应用程序 载入应用程式
Add Plotter	添加打印机		
Add Plotter	添加打印机	Apply	应用/申请 套用
Add to Favorites	添加到收藏夹 加入我的最爱	Approximation points	近似点
		Arc	圆弧 弧
ADI	Autodesk 设备接口 Autodesk 设备介面	Architectual Ticks	建筑标记 建筑斜线
		Area	区域，面积
		Argument	参数 引数
Adjacent	相邻	Arrange icons	排列图标 排列图示
Adjust	调整	Array	阵列
Adjust Area fill	调整区域填充 调整区域填满	Arrowhead	箭头
		ASCII ASCII	美国标准信息交换码
AdLM	Autodesk 许可管理器		
		Aseadmin	ASE 管理

Aseexport	ASE 输出 ASE 汇出	Azimuth	方位角 方位
Aselinks	ASE 链接 ASE 连结	Back Clipping On	后向剪裁打开
Aserows	ASE 行 ASE 列	Back view	后视图 后视景
Aseselect	ASE 选择 ASE 选取	Background color	背景色 背景颜色
Asesqled SQL	编辑 ASE SQL 编辑器	Backup	备份
		Backward	反向 左右反向
Aspect	纵横向间距	Bad	不正确的 不正确
Aspect ratio	宽高比 纵横比	Base	基点 基准,底端,底部
Assign	指定		
Assist	助理 辅助	Base dimension	基准标注 基线式标注
Associative dimension	关联标注 关联式标注		
		Base grips	基夹点 基准掣点
Associative hatches	关联填充 关联式剖面线	Base point	基点 基准点
		Baseline	基线 基准线 基线式
Attach	附着 贴附	Baseline dimension	基线标注 基线式标注
Attdef	属性定义		
Attdisp	属性显示	Basic color	基本色 基本颜色
Attedit	属性编辑 属性编辑	Batch plotting	批处理打印 批次出图
Attenuation	衰减 衰减		
Attenuation of light	灯光衰减 光源衰减	Beam angles of spotlights	聚光灯光束角度 点光源光线角度
Attext	属性提取 属性萃取		
Attredef	属性重定义 属性重新定义	Beep on Error	出错报警 错误时发出哔声
Attribute definition	属性定义	Bevel	倒角 斜切
Attribute Display	属性显示	Beveling objects	斜角对象 斜切物件
Attribute extraction file	属性提取文件 属性萃取档	Bezier curve	Bezier 曲线
		Big Font	大字体 大字体
Attribute extraction template file	属性提取样板文件 属性萃取样板档	Bind	绑定 并入
		Bitmap	位图 点阵图
		Blend	合成 混成
Attribute prompt	属性提示	Blipmode	点标记模式 点记模式
Attribute tag	属性标签		
Attribute value	属性值	Block	块 图块
Audit	核查 检核	Block definition	块定义 图块定义
Authorization code	授权码 授权码	Block reference	块参照 图块参考
AutoCAD library search path	AutoCAD库搜索路径 AutoCAD 资源库搜寻路径	Block table	块表 图块表格
		Bmpout	BMP 输出 BMP 汇出
Autocommit	自动提交 自动确定	Body	体 主体
AutoTrack	自动追踪 自动追踪	Boolean operation	布尔运算 布林运算
Axis tripod	三轴架 三向轴	Borders	边框 图框

Bottom view	仰视图 下视景	Check	检查
Boundary	边界	Check Box	复选框 勾选框
Boundary sets	边界集	Check Spelling	拼写检查 拼字检查
Bounding	边（框）边界框	Child dimension style	下级标注样式 子
Break	打断 切断		标注型式
Bring Above Object	置于对象之上 置	Chord	弦 翼弦
	于物件上方	Chprop	修改特性 变更性质
Bring to Top	顶置 置于最上方	Circle	圆
Brower	浏览器 浏览器	Circular external reference	循环外部参照 循
Built-in	内置的 内建		环外部参考
Bulge	凸度	Circumference	圆周
Bump map	凹凸贴图 凸纹贴图	Class	类 等级, 类别
Button menu	按钮菜单 按钮功	Clause	子句
	能表	Clean	清除
Bylock	随块	Clear	清除
Bylayer	随层	Client	客户机 用户端
Byte	字节 位元组	Clip	剪裁 截取
Cabling	电缆布线 配线	Clipboard	剪贴板 剪贴簿
Cal	计算器 校正	Clipping boundaries	剪裁边界 截取边界
Calibrate	校准 校正	Clipping planes	剪裁平面 截取平面
Call	调用 呼叫	Close	闭合 关闭(用于
Callback(for LISP)	回调 回覆		档案),闭合(用于
Callback	回叫 回覆		边界,线,面域)
Camera	相机 照相机	Cluster	组 丛集
Camera angle	相机角度 相机角度	Code pages	代码页 字码页
Cancel	取消	Color	颜色 著色
Cap	封口	Color depth	颜色深度
Cascade	层叠（的）重叠	Color map	色表 颜色对映
	排列	Color Wheel	颜色轮盘 色轮
Case	大小）写 大小写	Color-dependent	颜色相关
Cast	投射 投射	Color-Dependent Plot Style	颜色相关打印样
Catalog	目录	Table	式表
Cell	单元 储存格	Dangle	不固定的 悬挂
Center	圆心 中心	Dark Color	暗色
Center mark	圆心标记 中心点	Dash	虚线
	标记	Data integrity	数据完整性 资料
Centerline	中心线		完整性
Centroid	形心,质心 矩心	Database	数据库 资料库
Chamfer	倒角	Datum	基准 基准面
Change	修改 变更	Datum axis	基准轴
Character	字符 字元	Datum dimension	基准标注

Datum identifier	基准标识 基准识别字	dducsp UCS	方向对话框 动态 UCS 预设
Datum reference frames	基准参考框架 基准参考框	ddunits	单位对话框 动态单位设定
Datum reference letters	基准参考字母 基准参考文字	ddview	视图对话框 动态视景
DbConnect	数据库连接 资料库连结	ddvpoint	视点对话框 动态检视点
dbConnect Manager	数据库连接管理器	Deactivate	释放 停用
dblist	数据库列表 资料库列示	Dealer	经销商
		Decal effect	修剪效果 除去杂质效果
DBMS drivers	DBMS 驱动 资料库管理系统	Decimal dimensions	十进制标注 十进位标注
ddattdef	属性定义对话框 动态属性定义	Decurve	非曲线化 直线化
ddatte	属性编辑对话框 动态属性编辑	Default	缺省 预设值,预设
		Default drawing	缺省图形 预设图面
ddattext	属性提取对话框 动态属性萃取	Definition point	定义点
		Degenerate	退化
ddcolor	颜色对话框 动态颜色设定	Delay	延迟
		Delete	删除
ddedit	文字编辑对话框 编辑文字与属性定义	Delta	增量 差值
		Demand loading	按需加载 应要求载入
ddgrips	夹点对话框 动态掣点设定		
		Dependent symbols	依赖符号
ddim	标注设置对话框 标注设定	Deployment	展开 布署
		Depth Map	深度贴图 深度贴图
ddinsert	插入对话框 图块插入	Derive	导出
		Description	说明 描述
ddmodify	图元编辑对话框 动态修改	Design Center	设计中心 设计中心
		Detach	拆离 分离
ddptype	点类型对话框 点型式	Detection	检测 侦测
		Deviation	极限偏差 偏差
ddrename	重命名对话框 动态更名	Deviation tolerances	极限公差 偏差公差
		Device	设备
ddrmodes	绘图模式对话框 绘图设定	Device and Default Selection	设备和默认选择 设备和预设值选取
ddselect	对象选择对话框 动态选取设定	Dia	直径 直径
		Diameter	直径（标注）直径
dducs UCS	对话框 动态 UCS 设定	Dictionary	词典 字典
		Diffuse color	漫射色 漫射颜色

Digitizer	数字化仪 数位板	Direct Hatch	直接填充 直接剖面
Digitizing puck	数字化仪游标 数位化指向器	Direction Control	方向控制
Dim	标注	Directory	目录
Dimaligned	对齐标注 对齐式标注	Disable	禁用 取消,停用
		Discard	放弃 舍弃
Dimangular	角度标注	Discontinued	停止使用的 取消,停用
Dimbaseline	标注基线 基线式标注		
		Dish	下半球面 圆碟
Dimcenter	圆心标注 中心点标注	Disk space	磁盘空间 磁碟空间
		Displacement point	位移点 位移点
Dimcontinue	连续标注 连续式标注	Display	显示 显示器,显示,显示画面
Dimdiameter	直径标注	Display Order	显示次序 显示顺序
Dimedit	标注编辑	Dist	距离
Dimension	标注	Distant light	平行光 远光源
Dimension definition points	标注定义点	Distributing	分布 分散式
Dimension format	标注格式	Dithering	抖动 递色
Dimension geometry	构成要素标注几何	Diverge	分散的
Dimension line arc	尺寸线圆弧 标注线弧	Divide	等分
		Division	等分 分割,除法
Dimension properties	标注特性标注性质	Dock(undock)	固定（浮动）固定
Dimension scale	标注比例	Document	文档 文件
Dimension style	标注样式标注型式	Dome	上半球面 圆顶
Dimension style families	标注样式族 标注型式家族	Donut	园环 环
		Draft	草图
Dimension style name	标注样式名 标注型式名称	Drafting standards	绘图标准 制图标准
		Drafting techniques	绘图技术 制图技巧
Dimension style overrides	标注样式替代 标注型式取代	Drag and drop	拖放
		Draw	绘制/绘图 (如果后面未接宾语)
Dimension text	标注文字		绘图
Dimension units	标注单位		
Dimension variables	标注变量标注变数 线性标注	Drawing	图形 图面,图档
Dimlinear	线性标注	Drawing Aids	绘图辅助工具 绘图辅助
Dimordinate	坐标标注 座式标注		
		Drawing area	绘图区域 绘图区
Dimoverride	标注替代标注取代	Drawing boundaries	图形边界图面边界
Dimradius	半径标注	Drawing browser	图形浏览器 图面浏览器
Dimstyle	标注样式标注型式		
Dimtedit	标注文字编辑 标注文字编辑	Drawing database	图形数据库 图形资料库

Drawing environment	图形环境 绘图环境	Encapsulated	封装 See also
Drawing extents	图形范围 图面实		"EPS" 压缩
	际范围	End	端点 结束,终点
Drawing file	图形文件 图档	End angle	端点角度 结束角度
Drawing limits	图形界限 图面范围	End tangent	端点切向 结束切点
Drawing order	图形次序 绘图顺序	End width	端点宽度 结束宽度
Drawing project	图形项目 绘图专案	Ending	终止 端点
Drawing scale	图形比例 图面比例	English units	英制单位 英制
Drawing standard	图形标准 图面标准	Enter	输入
Drawing status	图形状态 图面状态	Entity	图元 元件 . 图元
Drawing time	绘图时间 绘图时间	Entry	条目 资料项
Drawing units	图形单位 图面单位	Environment	环境 环境
Driver	驱动程序 驱动程式	Environment variable	环境变量 环境变数
Dropdown List	下拉列表 下拉式	Equation	方程式
	列示	Erase	删除
Dsviewer	鸟瞰视图 鸟瞰视景	Existing	现有的 既有的
Dtext	动态文本 动态文字	Exit	退出 结束
Dump	转储 倾出	Export	输出 汇出
Duplicate	重复 重复的	Expression	表达式 表示式
Duplicating	复制	Extend	扩展 延伸
Dview	动态观察 动态检视	Extend	延伸，超出量（用
Dxbin	DXB输入 DXB		于标注）延伸
	汇入	Extension line	尺寸界线 延伸线
Dxfin	DXF输入 DXF 汇入	Extent(s)	范围 实际范围
Dxfout	DXF输出 DXF 汇出	External data	外部数据 外部资料
Dynamic	动态 动态	External database	外部数据库 外部
Dynamic Dragging	动态拖动 动态拖曳		资料库
Dynamic Update	动态更新 动态更新	External Reference	外部参照 外部参考
Dynamic viewing	动态观察 动态检视	Extract	选集 萃取
Dynamic zooming	动态缩放 动态缩放	Extrude	拉伸 挤出
Edge	边 边缘	Face	面
Edge Surface	边界曲面 边缘曲面	Facet	镶嵌面 产生刻面
Edgesurf	边界曲面 边缘曲面	Factor (see Scale Factor)	因子 系数
Editor	编辑器	Fade	褪色度 渐层
Education Version	教学版 教育版	Falloff angle	收缩角 衰退角度
Effect	效果	Fast Zoom mode	快速缩放模式 快
Element	元素		速缩放模式
Elev	标高 高程	Fatal	致命错误
Elevation	标高 高程	Favorites	收藏夹 我的最爱
Ellipse	椭圆	Feature	功能/（几何）特
Embed	内嵌，嵌入		征 特征

Fence (See also Selection fence)	栏选篱选	From	自
Field	字段 栏位	Front Clipping On	前向剪裁打开
File	文件 档案	Front view	主视图 前视景
Fill	填充 填实	Full Preview	全视口预览 完整
Filled Text	填充文字 文字填		预览
	实(用于填实线	General	基本 一般
	条、实体或实面)	Generate	生成 产生
Filmroll Filmroll	胶卷	Geometric characteristic	几何特性 几何特
Filter	过滤器	symbols	性符号
Find	查找 寻找工具	Geometric Tolerance	形位公差几何公差
Finish	完成 修饰	Geometry	几何图形几何图形
Finish（for render only）	修饰 修饰	Global	全局（的）整体
Fit	自适应设置 布满	Gouraud renderings Gouraud	着色 彩现
	（用于预览时，布	Gradient	百分度 渐层
	满视窗或图纸）	Grads	百分度 分度
Fit points	拟合点 拟合点	Graphic area	图形区 图形区
Flag	标志 旗标	Graphics cursor	图形光标图形游标
Flat Shaded, Edges on	带边框平淡着色	Graphics screen	图形屏 图形萤幕
Flat-shaded	（平淡）着色	Graphics window	图形窗口图形视窗
Floating viewports	浮动视口浮动视埠	Graphscr	图形屏 图形萤幕
Flood	布满 大量	Gray	灰度 灰阶
Flyout Properties	弹出特性对话框	Grid	网格 格点
	图示列性质	Grid	网格,栅格 格点
Fog	雾	Grid mode	栅格模式格点模式
Fold	折叠 折痕	Grip	夹点 掣点
Follow	跟随 自动平面视景	Group	编组 群组
Font	字体	Group code	组码 群组码
Font map file	字体映射文件 字	Haltftoning	半色调 半色调
	体对映档	Handle	句柄 处理码 (用
Form tolerance	形状公差成型公差		于性质对话方块)
Formatting text	设置文字格式 格		握手信号 交握
	式化文字	Handshaking	硬拷贝 硬体复制,
Frame	框架 画格		硬本
Frame	帧 画格	Hardcopy	硬件线型 硬体线型
Frame	边框 画格	Hardware linetype	保密锁 硬体锁
Free-form	自由形式（的）	Hardware lock	硬件需求 硬体需求
	自由形式	Hardware requirement	图案填充 剖面线
Freehand line	徒手画线 手绘线	Hatch	填充区域剖面区域
Freeplotting	自由绘图自由出图	Hatch areas	填充边界剖面边界
Freeze	冻结 冻结	Hatch boundaries	填充图案 剖面线
Freezing layers	冻结图层冻结图层		样式

Hatch pattern	填充样式 剖面样式	Internet Utilities Internet	应用程序 网际网路公用程式
Hatch styles	填充编辑 剖面线编辑	Interpolation points	插值点 内插点
Hatchedit	轻松设计抬头设计	Intersect	交集
Heads-up Design Icon	图标 图示	Interval	间距/间隔 间隔时间
Identifier	标识符 识别字		
IGES (International Graphics Exchange Specification)	初始图形交换标准 基本图形交换规格	Invalid	无效（的）无效
		Inverse linear attenuation of light	线性衰减 光线的线性反比衰减
Ignore	忽略	Inverse square attenuation of light	平方衰减 光线的平方反比衰减
Image	图像 影像		
Implement	实现 实施	Invisible	不可见
Import	输入 汇入	Invoke	调用 呼叫
Imprint	压印 盖印	Island	孤岛 孤立物件
Included angle	包含角 夹角	Island detection	孤岛检测 侦测孤立物件
Infinite lines	无限长线 无限长直线		
		ISO (International Standards Organization) ISO	ISO(国际标准化组织) ISO
Information	信息 资讯		
Inherit Properties	继承特性继承性质	Isolation levels	隔离级别 隔离层次
Initial environment	初始环境初始环境		
Initialize	初始化 起始设定	Isoline	素线 等角线
In-place	在位 现地	Isometric	等轴测 等角
Inquiry	查询	Isometric snap style	等轴测捕捉样式 等角锁点型式
Inscribed polygons	内接正多边形 内接多边形		
		Isometric view	等轴测视图 等角视景
Insert	插入		
Insertion	插入点	Isoplane	等轴测平面 等角平面
Insertobj	插入对象插入物件		
Instance	引用 实例	ISOPLANE	等轴测平面 等角平面
Instruction	指示		
Integer	整数	Italic	斜体 斜体
IntelliMouse	智能鼠标 智慧型滑鼠	Iterator	枚举器 重述子
		Join	合并 结合
Intensity	强度	Joint	连接 接合线
Interactive	交互的 互动式	Justification	对正 对正方式
Interchange	互换 交替	Justify	对正
Interface	介面	Key	主键
Interfere	干涉	Key	名称 主键
Interference	干涉	Knot vector	节点矢量要点向量
Interlace	隔行 交错	Label	标签
Internal	内部的 内部	Landscape	横向 横式

Landscape,if used for "landscape object" etc.	配景 风景 横式	Lineweight	线宽
		Link	链接 连结
Landscape Edit	编辑配景	List	表 串列
Landscape Library	配景库 景物图库	List	列表 串列
Lateral tolerance symbol	尺寸公差符号 侧向公差符号	List box	列表框 列示框
		List Files	文件列表
Layer index	图层索引 图层索引	Load	加载 载入
Layout	布局 配置	Locale	局部 本地
Layout from Template	来自样板的布局	Location (for Internet)	网址 位置
Layout from Template	来自样板的布局	Location (for file and directory)	位置
Layout Wizard	布局向导	Locked	锁定 锁护
Leader	引线	Locked layer	锁定图层锁护图层
Leading	前导	Logfileoff	关闭日志文件 关闭记录档
Learning Assistance	学习助手学习助理		
Left View	左视图 左视景	Logfileon	打开日志文件 开启记录档
Legacy	传统 旧式		
Length	长度	Logical	逻辑 逻辑的
Lengthen	拉长 调整长度	Long file name	长文件名 长档名
Lens Length	镜头长度镜头长度	Loop	环 回路
License Agreement	许可协议授权合约	LTSCALE	线型比例
License key	许可证号 授权码	Ltype	线型 线型
License Manager	许可管理器 授权管理员	Lump	块 小块
		Magnet	磁吸 磁铁
License Server	许可服务器 授权伺服器	Magnification	（缩放）比例倍率
		Magnifying glass	放大镜 放大境
Licenses	授权	Main window	主窗口 主视窗
Light	光源	Major axis	长轴
Light color (for RAMT-wood)	浅色 亮色	Make	新建 制作
Light Color	暖色 亮色	Make	建立 制作
Lighting	照明效果 照明	Malformed	有缺陷 畸形的
Lightness	亮度	Manipulate	操作 管理
Limits	图形界限 范围,图面范围	Manufacture	制造商
		Mapper	贴图
Line	行 线	Mapping	贴图,对映
Line	直线 线	Marble	大理石
Line font	线型 线字体	Mark	标记
Line object	线性对象 线物件	Massprop	质量特性质量性质
Line segment	线段	Match	匹配 相符
Line width	线宽	Material condition	包容条件材质条件
Linear Dimension	线性标注	Material condition symbols	包容条件符号 材质条件符号
Linetype	线型		

Materials	材质对话框 材质	Monochrome	单色（的）单色
Materials Library	材质库	Mouse	鼠标 滑鼠
Matlib	材质库	Move	移动
Measure	测量 测量	Mslide	制作幻灯 制作幻
Measure	等距等分（菜单		灯片
	内容）测量	Mspace	模型空间
Measurement	测量单位测量结果	Mtext	多行文字
MEASUREMENT	在图形中设置测	Multiline	多线比例 复线
	量值 测量结果	Multiline scale	多线比例复线比例
Member	成员	Multiline Style	多线样式复线型式
Memory	内存 记忆体	Mview	生成视口多重视埠
Menu	菜单 功能表	Mvsetup	设置图纸规格 多
Menu bar	菜单栏 功能表列		重视埠设定
Menuload	加载菜单 自订功	Named object	命名对象具名物件
	能表	Named plot style table	命名的打印样式
Merge	合并		表 具名的出图型
Message	信息 讯息		式表
Metafile	图元文件 中继档	Named UCS	命名UCS具名UCS
Method)	方法(用于物件导	Named view	命名视图 具名的
	向程式观念)		视景
Middle	中央点 中央	NE Isometric	东北等轴测 东北
Middle Center	正中点 正中		等角
Midpoint	中点	Nearest	最近点 最近点
Minsert	多重插入 插入图	Nested	嵌套 巢状式
	块阵列	Nested blocks	嵌套块巢状式图块
Mirror	镜像 镜射	New	新建 开新档案
Mirror line	镜像射线 镜射线	New Layout	新建布局
Mirror3d	三维镜像3D镜射	NURB surfaces NURBS	NURBS 曲面
Miscellaneous File Names	其他文件名 其它	NW Isometric	西北等轴测 西北
	档名		等角
Miter	斜接 斜接	Object	对象 物件
Mledit	多线编辑复线编辑	Object Properties	对象特性物件性质
Mline	多线 复线	Object Properties Manager	对象特性管理器
Mlstyle	多线样式复线型式		物件性质管理员
Mode	模式 模式	Object Snap	对象捕捉物件锁点
Model	型号 模型	Object snap override	对象捕捉覆盖 物
Model	建模，模型		件锁点取代
Model space	模型空间模型空间	Object Snap Setting	对象捕捉设置
Modification	修改	Objects	对象 物件
Monitor resolution	显示器分辨率 萤	Oblique	斜尺寸界线 倾斜
	幕解析度	Obsolete	废弃 旧式

ODBC database	数据库 ODBC 资料库	Override For dimension	替代 取代
Offset	偏移 偏移	Overwrite	覆盖 取代
OLE	(对象链接和嵌入)物件连接与嵌入(OLE)	Palette	控制板 选盘
		Palette	调色板 选盘
Olelinks	OLE链接 OLE 连结	Pan	平移
Online help	联机帮助线上说明	Pane	窗格
Online manuals	联机手册线上手册	Paper space	图纸空间
Oops	恢复 取消删除	Parameter	参数
Opacity map	不透明贴图 不透明贴图	Parent dimension style	上级标注样式 父系标注型式
Open	打开 开启 (大部分用于档案)	Parse	分析
		Partial	部分 局部
Open	打开(的) 开启 (大部分用于档案)	Partial Load	部分加载局部载入
		Password	口令 密码
OPM(Object Property Manager)	对象特性管理器	Paste Special	选择性粘贴 选择性贴上
Optimization	优化 最佳化	Pasteclip	粘贴 贴上截取
Option	选项 项	Pastespec	选择性粘贴 选择性贴上
Orbit	轨道 动态,动态检视	Path	路径
Ordinate	坐标标注 座标式	Pattern for "file search pattern"	方式 样式
Orientation	方向 方位	Pattern for hatch pattern, line pattern, etc.	图案 样式
Origin	原点（对于坐标系）原点	Pedit	多段线编辑 聚合线编辑
Origin (used for external Datebase)	原始位置原点		
Origin	起点（对于尺寸界线和标注）原点	Pen plotters	笔式绘图仪 笔式绘图机
Ortho	正交	Pen speed	笔速
Ortho mode	正交模式	Pen width	笔宽
Orthogonal	正交 正交的	Perfomance	性能
Orthographic	正交 正投影	Perimeter	周长
Osnap	对象捕捉物件锁点	Personalization	个人化
Outside	外部的 外侧 (用于文字位置)	Pface	复合面 聚合面
		Phong shading Phong	着色 描影
Overall dimension scale	全局比例 整体标注比例	Photo Raytrace renderer	照片级光线跟踪渲染 光线追踪相片彩现
Overflow (Compared tounderflow),	溢出 高溢 (相对于潜流),溢位	Photo Real renderer	照片级真实感渲染 真实相片彩现
Overlay	覆盖 覆叠		
Overline	上划线 顶线	Photo realistic rendering	照片级真实感渲染 相片质感彩现
Override For common sentences	忽略 取代		

Pick button	拾取键 点选钮	Polygon window	多边形窗口 多边形视窗
Pickbox	拾取框 点选框		
Pickfirst	选择优先 先点选	Polygonal clipping boundaries	多边形剪切边界 多边形截取边界
Picture	图片		
Pixel	像素	Polyline	多段线 聚合线
Placeholder	占位符 定位器	Polyline clipping boundaries	多段线裁剪边界 聚合线截取边界
Plan	平面图 平面		
Plan view	平面视图 平面视景	Polyline segments	多段线线段 聚合线线段
Planar projection	平面投影		
Pline	多段线 聚合线	Polymesh	多边形网格 聚合网面
Plot	打印 出图		
Plot Configuration	打印配置出图规划	Popup	弹出
Plot files	打印文件 出图档	Popup List	弹出列表弹出列示
Plot rotation	打印旋转出图旋转	Port	端口 埠
Plot spooling	打印假脱机 出图伫列	Portrait	肖像 直式
		Portrait，if used for paper layout	纵向 直式
Plot Style Manager	打印样式管理器	Positional tolerances	位置公差
Plot style table	打印样式表 出图型式表	Precision	精度 精确度
		Predefine	预定义 事先定义的
Plotter	绘图仪 绘图机	Preferences	系统配置环境设定
Plotter linetype	绘图仪线型 绘图机线型	Preferences dialog box	系统配置对话框 「环境设定」对话方块
Plotter Manager	打印机管理器		
Point Filters	点过滤 点过滤器	Preview	打印预览 预览
Point marker	点标记	Primitive	原型 基本原件
Point Sample	点采样 取样点	Priority	优先级 优先权
Point Style	点样式 点型式	Priviledge	特权 专用权
Pointer	指针	Procedural material	过程化材质 程序材质
Pointing device	定点设备 指向设备		
Polar array	环形阵列	Process	处理 程序
Polar coordinate	极坐标 极座标	Profile	配置/剖面(图)轮廓
Polar tracking	极轴追踪 极座标追踪	Program	编程 程式
		Projected tolerance zone	投影公差带 投影公差区
Polar tracking	极轴追踪 极座标追踪		
		Projected tolerances	投影公差投影公差
Polyface meshes	多面网格 聚合面网面	Prompt	提示
		Properties	特性 内容
Polygon	正多边形 多边形	Property painter	特性刷性质复制器
Polygon	多边形	Protocal	协议 通讯协定
Polygon meshes	多边形网格 多边形网面	Prototype	原型
		Proxy	代理

Proxy fonts	代理字体 代理字型	Reflection mapping	反射贴图 反射贴图
Pull down menu	下拉菜单 下拉功能表	Refractive index	折射指数 折射系数
		Refresh	刷新 更新
Purge	清理 清除	Regen	重生成 重生
Pyramid	棱锥面 三角锥体	Regenall	全重生成全部重生
QDIM	快速标注快速标注	Regenauto	自动重生成 自动
Qsave	快存 快速存档		重生
Qtext	快速文字	Regenerate	重生成 重生
Quadratic	二次	Regeneration	重生成 重生
Quality	质量 品质	Region	面域 面域
Quick Tour	快速指南 快速导览	Registry	注册表 登录
Radian	弧度 弪度	Reinit	重初始化 重新起
Radio Button	单选钮 圆钮		始设定
Radius	半径	Reinstall	重新安装重新安装
Raster file format	光栅文件格式 网格档案格式	Relative angles	相对角 相对角度
		Relative coordinates	相对坐标相对座标
Raster Image	光栅图像 网格式影像	Release	版本 版本
		Reload	重载 重新载入
Raster image boundaries	光栅图像边界 网格式影像边界	Remove	删除 移除
		Rename	重命名 更名
Ray	射线, 光线	Render	渲染 彩现
Ray Casting	射线法	Renderer	渲染程序 彩现程式
Raytraced renderer	光线跟踪渲染 光线追踪彩现	Replace	替换 取代
		Replay	重放 重播
Raytraced shadows	光线跟踪阴影 光线追踪阴影	Requirement	需求
		Reset	重置 重设
Read	读取	Resizing	改变大小 重新调
Realtime	实时 即时模式		整尺寸
Recover	恢复 修复	Resolution	融入 解析度
Rectang	矩形	Resolution	分辨率 解析度
Recursion	递归 递回	Restore	恢复 取回
Redefine	重定义 重新定义	Resume	恢复执行 继续执行
Redo	重做 重做	Retain	保留
Redraw	重画 重绘	Return button	回车键 Enter 键
Redrawall	全重画 全部重绘	Revert	复原 恢复原状
Reference	引用 参考	Revolve	旋转 回转
Reference	参照 参考	Revsurf	旋转曲面回转曲面
Reference angles	参考角 参考角度	Ridge	棱 脊线
Reference point	参考点	Right-Angle	直角
Refine	精度控制 精细化	Rmat	材质 彩现材质
Reflection color	反射色	Rollback	回卷 溯回

Root point	原点 根点	SE Isometric	东南等轴测 东南等角
Rotate	旋转		
Rotate3d	三维旋转 旋转3D	SE Isometric	东南等轴测 东南等角
Rotation	旋转		
Routine	例行程序 常式	Search for Help on	搜索帮助 寻找辅助说明主题
Rows dialog box	"行"对话框 列对话方块	Section	区域，部分，节(相对于章节)剖面
Rpref	渲染选项 彩现环境设定	Section	切割 剖面
Rscript	重复执行 重新执行脚本	Section	截面 剖面
		See	参见 参阅
Rubber-band line	拖引线 伸缩线	Segment	段，线段 区段，线段
Rulesurf	直纹曲面 规则曲面		
Run Script	运行脚本执行脚本	Select	选择 选取
Running object snap	执行对象捕捉 常驻式(物件锁点)	Select all	全部选择 全选
		Select object	对象选择 选取物件
Running override	整体替代整体取代	Selectable	可选择的 可选取
Runout	跳动 偏转度	Selection	选择集，选择选取选项(作名词用)
Sample	样例 取样		
Saturation	饱和度	Selection sets	选择集 选集
Save	保存 储存	Separate	分割 分隔,个别的
Save back	存回 回存	Serial number	序列号 序号
Saveas	另存为 另存新档	Session	任务 阶段作业
Saveimg	保存图像 储存影像	Set	设置，集合 设定
Scale if used as noun	比例缩放，（缩放）比例调整比例, 比例	Setting	设置 设定
		Shade (For monochrome Gray)	着色，灰度(用于单色Gray)描影
Scale factor	比例因子比例系数	Shader	着色程序 描影程式
Scaled to Fit	按图纸空间缩放调整比例到布满	Shadow map	阴影贴图
		Shape	形 造型
Scan	扫描	Sharpness	尖锐度 鲜明度
Scatter	散布图 散量	Sheet (for ACIS only)	表，板,图纸
Scene	场景	Shell	抽壳 薄壳
Schema	模式 纲要	Shell	薄壳
Schema	模式 纲要	Shell	抽壳 薄壳
Screen	屏幕 萤幕	Shortcut	快捷键 快显
Script	脚本	Show	显示 展示
Script files	脚本文件 脚本档	Silhouette	轮廓 剪影
Scroll bar	滚动条 卷动轴	Single Face	单一表面 单面
SDI(MDI)	单文档界面(多文档界面)	Single-pen plotter	单笔式绘图仪 单笔绘图机

Size	数目 尺寸	Splinedit	样条编辑 云形线编辑
Sizing	调整大小调整尺寸	Split	拆分 分割
Sketch	徒手画 徒手描绘	Spooler	缓冲（文件）排存器
Slice	剖切 切割面		
Slide	幻灯片	Spotlight angles	聚光灯角度
Slide libraries	幻灯库 幻灯片库	Stack	堆栈 堆叠
Smooth shading	平滑着色 平滑描影	Stack	堆叠
Smoothing angle	平滑角度	Stacked text	叠式文本堆叠文字
Snap	捕捉 锁点	Stamp	戳记
Snap angle	捕捉角度锁点角度	Standard	标准
Snap grid	捕捉栅格锁点格点	Start	起点 启动
Snap mode	捕捉模式锁点模式	Start angle	起点角度
Snap resolution	捕捉分辨率 锁点解析度	Start tangent	起点切向起始切点
		Start Up dialog box	"启动"对话框「启动」对话方
SnapTips	捕捉提示锁点提示		
Solid	填充 实体,2D实面	Starting	起始 起点
Solid	（二维）填充/（三维）实体 实体，2D实面	Statements	状态说明 叙述,.声明,陈述式
		Statistics	统计信息 统计值
Solid Fill	实体填充实面填实	Stats	统计 统计值
Solid modeler	实体建模 实体模型器	Status	状态
		Stlout STL	STL 输出 汇出
Solids	实体实体,3D实体	Stochastic	随机 推测
Sorting	排序	Stone Color	石质颜色石头颜色
Source applications	源文件	Straighten	拉直
Source point	源点 来源点	Stretch	拉伸
Space	空间	Strikeout Maybe	删去 删除线
Spacing	间距	Style	样式 字型
Special Edit	特定编辑 特殊编辑	Substitute	替换
Specific	指定（的）特定的	Subtract	差集 减去
Specific	特有的 特定的	Suffix	后缀 字尾
Specify	指定 指定	Support directory	支持目录支援目录
Specular reflection	镜面反射（高光）镜面反射	Support files	支持文件 支援档
		Suppress	禁止 抑制
Spelling	拼写检查 拼字	Suppress	不输出 抑制
Sphere	球面 圆球体	Suppress	收缩 抑制
Spherical projection	球面投影	Surface	曲面 表面
Spline	样条曲线 云形线	SW Isometric	西南等轴测 西南等角
Spline frame	样条曲线框架 云形线架构		
		Swap file	交换文件 置换档

环境艺术设计专业英语教程

Swatch	样本	Text editor	文本编辑器 文字编辑器
Sweep	延伸 扫掠		
Sweep	抹去 扫掠	Text fonts	字体
Sweep	扫掠	Text height	字高 文字高度
Switch	切换 开关	Text justification	文字对齐 文字对正
Switch	开关	Text properties	文字特性 文字性质
Swivel	旋转	Text style	文字样式 字型
Sym	符号	Textscr	文本屏 文字萤幕
Symbol set	符号集	Textual	文本（的）文字
Symbol table	符号表	Texture map	纹理贴图 材质贴图
Symmetrical	对称	Thaw	解冻
Synchronize	同步	Thickness	厚度
System requirements	系统需求 系统需求	Threshold	阈（值）临界值
System variables	系统变量 系统变数	Thumbnail	略图
Syswindows	系统窗口 系统视窗	Thumbnail preview image	略图预览图像 缩图预览影像
Tab	附签 标签		
Table	表 表格	Tick	标记 短斜线
Tablet	数字化仪 数位板	Tilde	波浪号 波浪符号（~）
Tabsurf	平移曲面 板展曲面		
Tabulated surface	平移曲面 板展曲面	Tile horizontal	水平平铺 非重叠 水平式
Tag	标记 标签		
Tangent	切线 切点	Tile vertical	垂直平铺
Tangential	相切 相切	Tiled viewports	平铺视口 非重叠视埠
Taper Faces	倾斜面 锥形面		
Tapered polyline segments	锥状多段线线段 锥状聚合线段	Tilemode	平铺模式 非重叠模式
Tapering	锥状 锥形	Tilemode	平铺模式 非重叠模式
Target	目标（点、对象）目标	Time	时间
Target box	靶框 目标框	Timeout	超时 逾时
Template drawing	样板图 样板图面	Title block	标题栏 标题栏
Temporary files	临时文件 暂存档	Toggle	开关，切换 切换
Terminate	终止 终止	Token	标记 记号
Tessellation lines	素线 镶嵌线	Tolerance	公差 公差
Tesslated text	嵌花文字	Toolbar	工具栏 工具列
Test	测试 测试	Top view	俯顶视图 上视景
Tetrahedron	四面体 四面体	Topology	拓扑结构 拓扑
Text，	文字，文本	Toroidal	环形 圆环形
Text color	文字色 文字颜色	Torus	圆环（体/面）圆环体
Text control codes	文字控制代码 文字控制码	Trace	宽线 追踪，等宽线

Trace	跟踪 追踪,等宽线	Video display	视频播放 视频显示器
Trailing	后续 结尾		
Transform	变换 转换	View	视图 视景
Translation	平移 转译	View Aligned	对齐浏览对齐视景
Transparency	透明 透明度	Viewpoint	视点 检视点
Transparent	图像透明度透通式	Viewport	视口 视埠
Transparent command	透明命令透通指令	Viewport configuration	视口配置视埠规划
Tree View	树状图	Viewres	显示精度 视景解析度
Treestat	树状结构 树构状态		
		Virtual screen display	虚屏显示 虚拟萤幕显示
Triangle	三角形		
Trim	修剪	Visibility	可见性 可见性
Tripod	三轴架 三向轴	Volumetric shadows	体积阴影体积阴影
Trunctuate	截短 截断	Vplayer	视口图层 视埠图层控制
Tube	管，圆管 圆管		
Turbulence	扰动 乱流	Vpoint	设置视点 检视点
Tutorials	教程 导览	Vports	多视口 视埠
Twist	扭曲 扭转	Vslide	观看幻灯 检视幻灯片
Type	类型 键入		
Ucsicon	UCS 图标 USC 图示	Warning	警告
		Wblock	写块 制作图块
Undefine	命令取消取消定义	Wedge	楔体表面 楔形体
Underflow	下溢 低溢	Weight	权值
Underline	下划线 底线	Weld	接合
Undo	放弃 复原	What's new	新特性 新增功能
Unhide	显示 取消隐藏	Width	宽度
Uninstall	删除安装 解除安装	Window	窗口 窗选
Union	并集 联集	Window polygon	窗口多边形 多边形窗选
Unload	卸载 释放		
Unnamed blocks	无名块 未具名块	Wire	连线 线素
Updating	更新 更新	Wireframe model	线框模型 线架构模型
Upside Down	倒置 上下颠倒		
User coordinate system(UCS)	用户坐标系使用者座标系统 (UCS)	Word wrap	词语换行 文字折行
		Working drawing	工作图形工作图面
Validation	校验 检验	World Coordinate System (WCS)	世界坐标系 世界座标系统
Variable	变量 变数		
Vector	矢量 向量	Xbind	外部参照绑定 外部并入
Vein Color	纹理颜色 纹路颜色		
Vertex	顶点	Xdata	外部数据 延伸资料
Vertical dimension	垂直标注	Xline	参照线 建构线
Vertices	顶点	Xplode	分解 炸开

Xef	外部参照 外部参考	Save As	存储为
Xref Log	外部参照记录文件 外部参考记录	Save for Web	存储为Web所用格式
Xref-dependent layer	依赖外部参照的图层	Revert	恢复
		Place	置入
Xref-dependent layer	依赖外部参照的图层	Import	输入
		PDF Image	PDF格式的图像
Xrefs (external references)	外部参照 外部参考	Annotations	注释
Zoom	缩放	Export	输出
Zoom limits	图限缩放 缩放范围	Manage Workflow	管理工作流程
Zoom Previous	缩放到上次 缩放前次	Check In	登记
		Undo Check Out	还原注销
Zoom window	按窗口，按作图区缩放 缩放窗选	Upload To Server	上载到服务器
		Add To Workflow	添加到工作流程
Height	高度	Open From Workflow	从工作流程打开
Help	帮助 说明	Automate	自动
Hidden Line	隐藏线	Batch	批处理
Hidden-line image	消隐图像 隐藏线影像	Create Droplet	创建快捷批处理
		Conditional Mode Change	条件模式更改
Hide	隐藏	Contact Sheet	联系表
Hide	消隐隐藏	Fix Image	限制图像
Hideplot	消隐出图 隐藏出图	Multi	多
Highlight	突出显示 亮显	Picture package	图片包
Highlight (for the color of 3D object)	亮光 (对颜色的三维物体) 亮显	Web Photo Gallery	网络图片库
		File Info	文件简介
Highlight	亮显	Print Options	打印选项
Home page	主页 首页	Page Setup	页面设置
Home position	起始位置 归位点	Print	打印
Hook line	钩线	Jump to	跳转到
Hotspot	聚光角 聚光点	Exit	退出
Hyperlink	超级链接 超连结	3.2 Edit	3.2编辑
3.PHOTO SHOP Chinese and English comparison	3. PHOTO SHOP中英文对照	Undo	还原
		Step Forward	向前
		Step Backward	返回
3.1 File	3.1 文件	Fade	消退
New	新建	Cut	剪切
Open	打开	Copy	拷贝
Open As	打开为	Copy Merged	合并拷贝
Open Recent	最近打开文件	Paste	粘贴
Close	关闭	Paste Into	粘贴入
Save	存储	Clear	清除

附 环境景观专业术语

Fill	填充	Duotone	双色调
Stroke	描边	Indexed Color	索引色
Free Transform	自由变形	RGB Color	RGB色彩
Transform	变换	CMYK Color	CMYK颜色
Again	再次	Lab Color	实验室彩色
Sacle	缩放	Multichannel	多通
Rotate	旋转	8 Bits/Channel	8位通
Skew	斜切	16 Bits/Channel	16位通
Distort	扭曲	Color Table	颜色表
Prespective	透视	ssing Profile	制定配置文件
Rotate 180°	旋转180度	Convert to Profile	转换为配置文件
Rotate 90° CW	顺时针旋转90度	Adjust	调整
Rotate 90° CCW	逆时针旋转90度	Levels	色阶
Flip Hpeizontal	水平翻转	Auto Laves	自动色阶
Flip Vertical	垂直翻转	Auto Contrast	自动对比度
Define Brush	定义画笔	Curves	曲线
Define Pattern	设置图案	Color Balance	色彩平衡
Define Custom Shape	定义自定形状	Brightness/Contrast	亮度/对比度
Purge	清除内存数据	Hue/Saturation	色相/饱和度
Undo	还原	Desaturate	去色
Clipboard	剪贴板	Replace Color	替换颜色
Histories	历史纪录	Selective Color	可选颜色
All	全部	Channel Mixer	通道混合器
Color Settings	颜色设置	Gradient Map	渐变映射
Preset Manager	预置管理器	Invert	反相
Preferences	预设	Equalize	色彩均化
General	常规	Threshold	阈值
Saving Files	存储文件	Posterize	色调分离
Display&Cursors	显示与光标	Variations	变化
Transparency&Gamut	透明区域与色域	Duplicate	复制
Units&Rulers	单位与标尺	Apply Image	应用图像
Guides&Grid	参考线与网格	Calculations	计算
Plug	插件	Image Size	图像大小
Memory&Image Cache	内存和图像高速缓存	Canvas Size	画布大小
		Rotate Canvas	旋转画布
Adobe Online	Adobe公司在线	180°	180度
Workflows Options	工作流程选项	90° CW	顺时针90度
Image	图像	90° CCW	逆时针90度
Mode	模式	Arbitrary	任意角度
Bitmap	位图	Flip Horizontal	水平翻转
Grayscale	灰度	Flip Vertical	垂直翻转

Crop	裁切	Gradient	渐变
Trim	修整	Pattern	图案
Reverl All	显示全部	New Adjustment Layer	新调整图层
Histogram	直方图	Levels	色阶
Trap	陷印	Curves	曲线
Extract	抽出	Color Balance	色彩平衡
Liquify	液化	Brightness/Contrast	亮度/对比度
3.4 Layer	3.4图层	Hue/Saturation	色相/饱和度
New	新建	Selective Color	可选颜色
Layer	图层	Channel Mixer	通道混合器
Background From Layer	背景图层	Gradient Map	渐变映射
Layer Set	图层组	Invert	反相
Layer Set From Linked	图层组来自链接的	Threshold	阈值
Layer via Copy	通过拷贝的图层	Posterize	色调分离
Layer via Cut	通过剪切的图层	Change Layer Content	更改图层内容
Duplicate Layer	复制图层	Layer Content Options	图层内容选项
Delete Layer	删除图层	Type	文字
Layer Properties	图层属性	Create Work Path	创建工作路径
Layer style	图层样式	Convert to Shape	转变为形状
Blending Options)	混合选项	Horizontal	水平
Drop Shadow	投影	Vertical	垂直
Inner Shadow	内阴影	Anti-Alias None	消除锯齿无
Outer Glow	外发光	Anti-Alias Crisp	消除锯齿明晰
Inner Glow	内发光	Anti-Alias Strong	消除锯齿强
Bevel and Emboss	斜面和浮雕	Anti-Alias Smooth	消除锯齿平滑
Satin	光泽	Covert To Paragraph Text	转换为段落文字
Color Overlay	颜色叠加	Warp Text	文字变形
Gradient Overlay	渐变叠加	Update All Text Layers	更新所有文本图层
Pattern Overlay	图案叠加	Replace All Missing Fonts	替换所以缺欠文字
Stroke	描边	Rasterize	栅格化
Copy Layer Effects	拷贝图层样式	Type	文字
Paste Layer Effects	粘贴图层样式	Shape	形状
Paste Layer Effects To Linked	将图层样式粘贴的链接的	Fill Content	填充内容
		Layer Clipping Path	图层剪贴路径
Clear Layer Effects	清除图层样式	Layer	图层
Global Light	全局光	Linked Layers	链接图层
Create Layer	创建图层	All Layers	所以图层
Hide All Effects	显示/隐藏全部效果	New Layer Based Slice	基于图层的切片
Scale Effects	缩放效果	Add Layer Mask	添加图层蒙板
New Fill Layer	新填充图层	Reveal All	显示全部
Solid Color	纯色	Hide All	隐藏全部

Reveal Selection	显示选区	Inverse	反选
Hide Selection	隐藏选区	Color Range	色彩范围
Enable Layer Mask	启用图层蒙板	Feather	羽化
Add Layer Clipping Path	添加图层剪切路径	Modify	修改
Reveal All	显示全部	Border	扩边
Hide All	隐藏全部	Smooth	平滑
Current Path	当前路径	Expand	扩展
Enable Layer Clipping Path	启用图层剪切路径	Contract	收缩
Group Linked	于前一图层编组	Grow	扩大选区
UnGroup	取消编组	Similar	选区相似
Arrange	排列	Transform Selection	变换选区
Bring to Front	置为顶层	Load Selection	载入选区
Bring Forward	前移一层	Save Selection	存储选区
Send Backward	后移一层	3.6 Filter	3.6滤镜
Send to Back	置为底层	Last Filter	上次滤镜操作
Arrange Linked	对齐链接图层	Artistic	艺术效果
Top Edges	顶边	Colored Pencil	彩色铅笔
Vertical Center	垂直居中	Cutout	剪贴画
Bottom Edges	底边	Dry Brush	干笔画
Left Edges	左边	Film Grain	胶片颗粒
Horizontal Center	水平居中	Fresco	壁画
Right Edges	右边	Neon Glow	霓虹灯光
Distribute Linked	分布链接的	Paint Daubs	涂抹棒
Top Edges	顶边	Palette Knife	调色刀
Vertical Center	垂直居中	Plastic Wrap	塑料包装
Bottom Edges	底边	Poster Edges	海报边缘
Left Edges	左边	Rough Pastels	粗糙彩笔
Horizontal Center	水平居中	Smudge Stick	绘画涂抹
Right Edges	右边	Sponge	海绵
Lock All Linked Layers	锁定所有链接图层	Underpainting	底纹效果
Merge Linked	合并链接图层	Watercolor	水彩
Merge Visible	合并可见图层	Blur	模糊
Flatten Image	合并图层	Blur More	进一步模糊
Matting	修边	Gaussian Blur	高斯模糊
Define	去边	Motion Blur	动态模糊
Remove Black Matte	移去黑色杂边	Radial Blur	径向模糊
Remove White Matte	移去白色杂边	Smart Blur	特殊模糊
3.5 Selection	3.5 选择	Brush Strokes	画笔描边
All	全部	Accented Edges	强化边缘
Deselect	取消选择	Angled Stroke	成角的线条
Reselect	重新选择	Crosshatch	阴影线

Dark Strokes	深色线条	Sharpen More	进一步锐化
Ink Outlines	油墨概况	Unsharp Mask	USM锐化
Spatter	喷笔	Sketch	素描
Sprayed Strokes	喷色线条	Bas Relief	基底凸现
Sumi	烟灰墨	Chalk & Charcoal	粉笔和炭笔
Distort	扭曲	Charcoal	木炭
Diffuse Glow	扩散亮光	Chrome	铬黄
Displace	置换	Conte Crayon	彩色粉笔
Glass	玻璃	Graphic Pen	绘图笔
Ocean Ripple	海洋波纹	Halftone Pattern	半色调图案
Pinch	挤压	Note Paper	便条纸
Polar Coordinates	极坐标	Photocopy	副本
Ripple	波纹	Plaster	塑料效果
Shear	切变	Reticulation	网状
Spherize	球面化	Stamp	图章
Twirl	旋转扭曲	Torn Edges	撕边
Wave	波浪	Water Paper	水彩纸
Zigzag	水波	Stylize	风格化
Noise	杂色	Diffuse	扩散
Add Noise	加入杂色	Emboss	浮雕
Despeckle	去斑	Extrude	突出
Dust & Scratches	蒙尘与划痕	Find Edges	查找边缘
Median	中间值	Glowing Edges	照亮边缘
Pixelate	像素化	Solarize	曝光过度
Color Halftone	彩色半调	Tiles	拼贴
Crystallize	晶格化	Trace Contour	等高线
Facet	彩块化	Wind	风
Fragment	碎片	Texture	纹理
Mezzotint	铜版雕刻	Craquelure	龟裂缝
Mosaic	马赛克	Grain	颗粒
Pointillize	点状化	Mosained Tiles	马赛克拼贴
Render	渲染	Patchwork	拼缀图
3D Transform	3D变换	Stained Glass	染色玻璃
Clouds	云彩	Texturixer	纹理化
Difference Clouds	分层云彩	Video	视频
Lens Flare	镜头光晕	De	逐行
Lighting Effects	光照效果	NTSC Colors	NTSC颜色
Texture Fill	纹理填充	Other	其它
Sharpen	锐化	Custom	自定义
Sharpen	锐化	High Pass	高反差保留
Sharpen Edges	锐化边缘	Maximum	最大值

Minimum	最小值	Guides	参考线
Offset	位移	Grid	网格
Digimarc	水印	Slices	切片
Embed Watermark	嵌入水印	Document Bounds	文档边界
Read Watermark	读取水印	All	全部
3.7 View	3.7视图	None	无
New View	新视图	Show Guides	锁定参考线
Proof Setup	校样设置	Clear Guides	清除参考线
Custom	自定	new Guides	新参考线
Working CMYK	处理CMYK	Lock Slices	锁定切片
Working Cyan Plate	处理青版	Clear Slices	清除切片
Working Magenta Plate	处理洋红版	3.8 Windows	3.8窗口
Working Yellow Plate	处理黄版	Cascade	层叠
Working Black Plate	处理黑版	Tile	拼贴
Working CMY Plate	处理CMY版	Arrange Icons	排列图标
Macintosh RGB	苹果RGB	Close All	关闭全部
Windows RGB	视窗RGB	Show/Hide Tools	显示/隐藏工具
Monitor RGB	显示器RGB	Show/Hide Options	显示/隐藏选项
Simulate Paper White	模拟纸白	Show/Hide Navigator	显示/隐藏导航
Simulate Ink Black	模拟墨黑	Show/Hide Info	显示/隐藏信息
Proof Color	校样颜色	Show/Hide Color	显示/隐藏颜色
Gamut Wiring	色域警告	Show/Hide Swatches	显示/隐藏色板
Zoom In	放大	Show/Hide styles	显示/隐藏样式
Zoom Out	缩小	Show/Hide History	显示/隐藏历史记录
Fit on Screen	满画布显示	Show/Hide Actions	显示/隐藏动作
Actual Pixels	实际象素	Show/Hide Layers	显示/隐藏图层
Print Size	打印尺寸	Show/Hide Channels	显示/隐藏通道
Show Extras	显示额外的	Show/Hide Paths	显示/隐藏路径
Show	显示	Show/Hide Character	显示/隐藏字符
Selection Edges	选区边缘	Show/Hide Paragraph	显示/隐藏段落
Target Path	目标路径	Show/Hide Status Bar	显示/隐藏状态栏
Grid	网格	Reset Palette Locations	复位调板位置
Guides	参考线	**Five. Terminology used**	**五. 家具常用专**
Slices	切片	**furniture**	**业术语**
Notes	注释	wooden furniture	木家具
All	全部	bookshelf	书架
None	无	metal furniture	金属家具
Show Extras Options	显示额外选项	flower-stand	花架
Show Rulers	显示标尺	plastic furniture	塑料家具
Snap	对齐	hatrack	帽架
Snap To	对齐到	bamboo furniture	竹家具

clothes-hanger	衣架	vertical aividing partition	中隔板
rattan furniture	藤家具	closet	壁橱
newspaper rack	报架	shelf	层板、搁板
frame-type furniture	框式家具	cupboard	橱柜
magazine rack	杂志架	pivoted door	开门
panel-type furniture	板式家具	dressing table, dresser	梳妆台
screen, folding screen	屏风	overhead door, up and over	翻门
combination furniture	组合家具	door, swing-up door, flap	
door	门	counter	柜台
bentwood furniture	曲木家具	sliding door	移门
mirror	镜	desk	课桌
folding furniture	折迭家具	multifolding door	卷门
shutters	百叶窗	folding table	折迭桌
wardrobe	衣柜	top	顶板
windowsill	窗台	adjustable bed	可调床
chest of drawers	五斗柜	top	面板
staircase	楼梯	double-bed	双人床
bedside(cabinet), night stand	床头柜	bottom	底板
lobby	走廊	single-bed	单人床
filing cabinet	文件柜	back	背板
single room	单人房间	bunk	双层床
sideboard, buffet	餐柜	apron	望板、围板
double room	双人房间	child cot or baby crib	童床
cocktail cabinet	吧柜、酒柜	base	脚架
bed board	床板	corner table	角几
dining car	餐车	base	脚盘
bedstead	床架	tea-table or coffee-table or	茶几
display cabinet	陈设柜	end table	
side	侧板	drawer	抽屉
wall units	组合柜	teaboard	茶盘
headboard	床头板	leg	脚
bookcase	书柜	sofa	沙发
bedspread	床罩	ceiling	天花板
T.V cabinet	电视柜	wooden arms sofa	木扶手沙发
doorframe	门框	pillow	枕头、枕垫
shoes cabinet	鞋柜	upholstered sofa	全包沙发
doorplante, tablet, house	门牌	bed sheet	被单
number plate		sofa bed	两用沙发
desk	书台	mattress	床垫
picture frame	镜框	chair	椅子
dining table	餐台	pelmet	窗帘盒

armchair	扶手椅
cushion	垫子
swivel chair	转椅
rug	小地毯
rocking chair	摇椅
carpet	大地毯
folding chair	折椅
wicker chair	藤椅
high chair	高脚椅
barstool	吧椅
bench, stool	凳
foot-stool	踏脚凳
round table	圆桌

图6-1 普通驳岸
Fig.6-1 Ordinary Revetment

图6-2 缓坡驳岸
Fig.6-2 Revetment with Gentle Slopes

图6-3 带河岸群墙的驳岸
Fig.6-3 Revetment with River Banks and Walls

图6-4 阶梯驳岸
Fig.6-4 Revetment With Steps

图6-5 带平台的驳岸
Fig.6-5 Revetment with Platforms

图6-6 缓坡、阶梯复合驳岸
Fig.6-6 Revetment with Gentle Slopes and Steps

图6-7 钢制桥
Fig.6-7 Steel Bridge

图6-8 混凝土桥
Fig.6-8 Concrete Bridge

图6-9 拱桥
Fig.6-9 Arch Bridge

图6-10 原木桥
Fig.6-10 Log Bridge

图6-11 仿木桥
Fig.6-11 Imitation Wood Bridge

图6-12 锯材木桥
Fig.6-12 Lumber Wood Bridge

图6-13 吊桥
Fig.6-13 Suspension Bridge

图6-14 邻水木栈道
Fig.6-14 Plank Road Above Water

图6-15 滨水木栈道
Fig.6-15 Plank Road Along Water

图6-16 滑落式
Fig.6-16 Slide Waterfall

图6-17　阶梯式
Fig.6-17　Step Waterfall

图6-18　幕布式
Fig.6-18　Curtain Waterfall

图6-19　丝带式
Fig.6-19　Ribbon Waterfall

图6-20　可涉入式
Fig.6-20　Wading Style

图6-21　不可涉入式
Fig.6-21　Non-Wading Style

图6-22　生态水池
Fig.6-22　Ecological Pool

图6-23　热带生态水池
Fig.6-23　Tropic Ecological Pool

图6-24　中式庭院式泳池
Fig.6-24　Chinese-style Swimming-pool

图6-25 西式庭院式泳池
Fig.6-25 Western-style Swimming-pool

图6-26 人工海滩
Fig.6-26 Artificial Beach

图6-27 泰姬陵
Fig.6-27 Taj Mahal

图6-28 壁泉
Fig.6-28 Wall Fountain

图6-29 涌泉
Fig.6-29 Stave Fountain

图6-30 旱地喷泉
Fig.6-30 Dry Land Fountain

图6-31 跳泉
Fig.6-31 Leap Fountain

图6-32 雾化喷泉
Fig.6-32 Spray Fountain